the seer

the mind of the entrepreneur,

artist,

visionary,

innovator,

seeker,

learner,

leader,

creator,

...you

The Seer

the mind of the entrepreneur, artist, visionary, innovator, seeker, learner, leader, creator...you

David Robinson

Tweet This Book!

Please help David Robinson by spreading the word about this book on Twitter!

The suggested hashtag for this book is #theseer.

Find out what other people are saying about the book by clicking on this link to search for this hashtag on Twitter:

https://twitter.com/search?q=#theseer

For Marcia Lou & Tom McKenzie. Mentors. Guides.
Friends.

Contents

CONTENTS

Foreword

David Robinson is a gift. If you have worked with him as a consultant, coach, facilitator, artist, director, collaborator, or performer, or have known him as a friend, then you know this already. We first met in 2006—a hurried introduction through a mutual friend in another friend's kitchen in Northern California. Little did we know then that this half-hour encounter would set the tone for our deep friendship and rich collaboration.

Though we entered that kitchen as strangers, within five minutes we were in deep and profound creative dialogue. It felt like magic. Our mutual friend sat in amazement as he watched the two of us "riffing" off of each other, already building the framework of what has become a deep and cherished friendship and partnership. Even all these years later, we actually know very little about one another's day-to-day lives. In fact, until very recently we've lived on opposite coasts of the U.S. and still remain a time zone apart. We've been in the same room together less than dozen times. Yet we know the depths of one another's hearts and souls intimately. Our frequent telephone calls and rare face-to-face meetings follow the same pattern as our first encounter. Within five minutes we have taken a deep dive into discovery and creation. We serve as witnesses for one another's successes, challenges, growth, and transformation as we paddle the winding rivers of our lives. This is the gift that David Robinson is to me.

While David and I have explored the concepts and principles presented in The Seer a thousand times and taught them in various forms in the Transformational Presence programs, I get excited and inspired all over again as I read this book. Transformation happens at the most fundamental levels of being, thinking, and belief. We can't make it happen—that's called "manipulation!" However, we can create the best possible conditions for the transformation to unfold. Think of it as planting a garden. There is absolutely nothing you can do to make the seeds grow. However, there are many things you can do to encourage and support their growth. You can choose a spot that will get just the right amount of sunlight. You can plant the seeds in rich, fertile soil, and then make sure they have just the right amount of water. You can keep the garden free of weeds to ensure that the young plants have room to breathe and grow.

It's the same with transformation. We can't make it happen, but we can create the best possible environment for it to unfold. Creating that environment begins with learning to see, perceive, and think in new ways. Once we can see beyond our preconceptions, beliefs, thoughts, and habitual ways of doing things, a new world opens to us. Things that we never imagined possible are suddenly within reach. It's just a matter of approach, and it's easier than you think.

Part of David's brilliance lies in his ability to see things as story. He masterfully weaves together archetypal stories and great wisdom teachings to shed new light on current life circumstances. Through his brilliant storytelling, David invites compassion and understanding for our own circumstance, while at the same time nudging us forward. Well, sometimes it feels more like a swift kick in the pants! Nevertheless, we receive clear insights about what wants to shift within our own stories and recognize a path forward.

Through The Seer, David leads us back to our fundamental worldviews about how life works. He takes us on a journey to realign our thoughts, beliefs, and actions with our greatest potential so that we might realize our dreams, make the contributions we are here to make, and serve in the ways we feel called to serve.

For many, this book will be eye opening. Others might say there is nothing new here—no concept or idea that they haven't heard or read before. However the book feels to you, I invite you to step beyond what you think you know already. Read from your heart and your mind will follow. You might be surprised to find new levels of understanding that you haven't realized before. David presents these concepts in ways that you can really "get them" and also sense how to apply them.

Finally, this is an interactive book. You have to do your part. Take time for the tasks at the end of each "Recognition." Let this book be your transformation partner and you will experience shifts in perception. You will stretch beyond the limits of your present thinking, your beliefs, and perhaps even your culture.

Becoming a "seer" is an important step toward freedom, success, and fulfillment. It is a critical step in learning to create in new ways. Take the step. A new world awaits.

Alan Seale

Director, Center for Transformational Presence[1] Author of *Create A World That Works* and *The Manifestation Wheel*

---

[1]http://transformationalpresence.org

Acknowledgments

I am deeply indebted to Skip Walter. This book would not have happened without our rich collaboration, friendship, the hours of mad scribbling we spent in front of a whiteboard, and multiple adventures into the world of wine. In fact, I owe a debt of gratitude to the entire Walter clan, Jamie and Maggie in particular, for their hours of editing, formatting, and feedback. I could not have had a better support team.

I am grateful for Megan Longshore for slapping me awake, helping me clarify my thoughts, and her insistence that I learn to take smaller steps. Additionally, many thanks to the amazing educators and community of Hastings, Nebraska for their courage, their willingness to jump into experiences, and generous support that helped me fully explore my ideas.

Thank you also to Tori Grace for your gift of story, your cartoons, and wild imagination.

As always, thanks to Alan Seale for years of collaboration and warm friendship. Our ongoing work is an ever-present source of inspiration and guidance.

Finally, to Kerri Sherwood for your love, guidance, patience, editing-eyes, heart-song, endless encouragement and support, I am deeply grateful.

How To Use This Book

Entrepreneurs, artists, visionaries, innovators, learners, creators, leaders and seekers operate from a different mindset than most people; they see through different eyes. This book is intended to shift your mindset so you might see through entrepreneurial eyes.

Shifting a mindset is a dynamic process, not an intellectual exercise. A dynamic process requires an engagement with the day-to-day experiences of life and, therefore, requires two universal and necessary tools:

1. A Reflective Practice. Processes of self-knowledge are tricky because you are both the subject of the study and the studier. You are attempting to raise your conscious awareness of patterns of thinking and acting. You are sitting on the mountain so you can't see it. *A reflective practice is necessary to see the mountain upon which you sit.* In The Artist's Way this practice was called morning pages. In some processes it is called journaling. In others it goes by the name of reflective writing or free writing. Whatever you wish to call it or however you want to do it, it is an essential tool in opening your eyes to existing patterns and entrenched beliefs. Reflective writing is the best way for you to talk to yourself, to get beyond the moat of what you think you know and discover the deeper story structure driving your actions.

2. Pattern Breaking. In order to release your grip on what you think you know, to shake up your comfort and control, you need to break habits and patterns and break them intentionally. And, it is better if you have fun doing it. This is the equivalent of the artist's date. Sometimes this is called stirring the pot, breaking habits, or giving your self a gift. Regardless of the name it is necessary to challenge your assumptions if you want to open your mind and your eyes to new ways of seeing. Breaking patterns will help surface essential bits to write about in your reflective practice. It's a feedback loop.

The form of your reflective practice and pattern breaking is less important than the *consistency* of doing it. Give yourself time to reflect every day so that you may uncover your daily patterns of thinking and seeing. Use the tools, devices, and practices introduced in the book to consciously break your patterns. See what happens. Write about it.

Through the story you will move through 9 Recognitions. Each Recognition is followed by 3 tasks:

1) A Study

2) An Action

3) An Exercise

The tasks will help you develop new patterns of thinking and seeing. To that end, you will also find within the narrative a few related practices. The practices are useful in preparing your mind for the flip to a new way of thinking. This process is like riding a bike: you can read about it and trick yourself into believing that you know what to do - or you can get on the bike, start pedaling, fall down a few times and learn to ride. In other words, the practices and tasks will only help if you do them; they can't help if you don't engage with them. To reiterate: perspective shifts are not an intellectual exercise; they are dynamic processes. Shifts in perspective are intuitive, experiential *engagements* made conscious through action and reflection. Entrepreneurs, innovators, and life learners are artists: they engage in dynamic, fluid creative practices. So, get on the bike and ride. Challenge what you think you know. Open your eyes to possibilities. Allow yourself to make meaning of your experiences *after* you have them. It is, after all, how your brain works so you might as well begin by dropping the illusion that you know something before you encounter it - it's an important skill for a creator in any field or profession.

Finally, although this may seem counterintuitive, at the core, artists and entrepreneurs must master two skills:

1) Pattern Recognition

2) Metaphor

Serial entrepreneur, Ash Bhoopathy said it best: "The more you see, the more you see patterns." Mastering pattern recognition is about mastering seeing and vice versa. After you learn to see your patterns, you become capable of seeing beyond your patterns into your field of opportunity. Then, a magic perspective shift happens: you begin to see that no one creates in a vacuum. No one innovates, leads, learns, or grows by themselves. Creativity is a group sport. Everyone shares the same field of opportunity! This "creative commons" is the province of metaphor. "Mastering metaphor," according to Ash, is this: "making the familiar strange and/or making the strange familiar." Can you imagine a more important capacity in the development, marketing, and sales of a product or service? Can you imagine a better definition of learning? Can you imagine a better reason to pursue artistry? Make the familiar strange. Make the strange familiar. Learn to see.

To support your progress toward mastery of pattern recognition and metaphor, an ancient tale is braided through this narrative.

To recap: the path to an entrepreneurial mindset is through the mastery of pattern recognition and metaphor. Mastery is made possible through two simple actions: intentional pattern breaking and a reflective practice. It's a feedback loop.

Prologue

This is a book about seeing.

Not many people see. Most people merely look. Just as most people hear but they do not listen, most people look but they do not see.

And, although this might not make sense yet, seeing has more to do with stories than it does with eyes. It works like this:

Everyone can see as a child. And then something happens.

Children learn to name things with words. Then they learn to spell the words they use to name things. Soon they grow up and have a hard time seeing beyond their words. Often they name their experiences before they even have them. They do not see what is there, they see what they *think* is there.

It is a funny paradox about words - they can imprison your mind. Words can also set you free. It all depends upon how the words are used.

Entrepreneurs and artists share this trait: in order to master their craft they must learn to see again. And, in order to see, they must once again understand the power of their words; they must learn to see beyond their story. They must learn to flip their assumptions and let go of what they think they know.

Cycle One: Pattern

Recognition 1: You don't have a problem. You have a pattern.

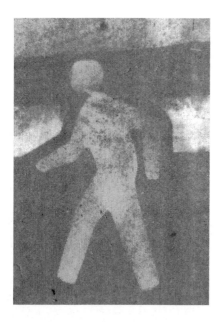

1.

Some cultures actually believe that stories stalk you. They believe that a story is given to you before you are ready to hear it and then the story follows you throughout your life. Stories are patient and will stalk you for years. When it is first given, you miss the meaning of it or perhaps only understand the most superficial layer. So, like your shadow, the story walks with you waiting for the moment that you need it most. At that very moment, it penetrates your being. It becomes you. You become the story.

That is certainly true of the story of Parcival and me. When I was a kid I brought home a big picture book of mythology. In it was the story of Parcival. I loved it. It is a story of determination and passion. It is a story of ambition and service. I was captivated by Parcival's desire to make a better world for people. I loved his unwavering pursuit of his dream. I loved how different he was from all of the other knights. He made his own path. His path was entrepreneurial. I read every version of the story that I could find.

Like all the stories that wound up in the Round Table, I learned that Parcival's story is ancient, predating Christianity by hundreds of years. Parcival was the most unusual of King Arthur's knights. His story stalked me for years, so well in fact, that I didn't even know that it was following right behind me all through college, while I was creating my business and following my passions. And then, one day when everything collapsed, when my business tanked and my dream dissolved, when I needed the story the most, it stepped forward and took me. Since that day I have never seen the world or my work in the same way.

2.

He insisted that we work through online chat. No phone calls. No video. I thought it was odd but Virgil came highly recommended to me so I decided not to resist his preference. This was our first contact and I had just finished describing my business problems.

> **Virgil**: You don't know what you don't know.

I stared at the screen and thought, "That's not very helpful."

I had contacted him because I was tired of failing. I felt stuck. I felt like I was working all the time and somehow always ended back in the same place: at zero and broke. I had good ideas, some great ideas for new products and services and yet I was once again at zero. My latest business collapsed just as the one before it. I was certain my latest venture was the one. I was certain. I brought my best game and still I failed. What was I doing wrong?

His next message popped onto the screen.

> **Virgil**: You think as everyone thinks, that you simply need to change what you are doing and that will solve all of your problems. You think there is a prescription. That kind of thinking will only lead you back to zero.

I was getting frustrated. I was desperate. I needed to change. I needed to know what to do differently and I needed to know now. I needed to know! I've always known what to do but now I was lost. I was in no mood for mumbo-jumbo philosophy.

> **Virgil**: From what you wrote, I see that you think you have a problem. The first recognition is simple: you do not have a problem. You have a pattern.

I closed my eyes and pinched the bridge of my nose. A pattern? That's it? That's the best this guy could offer me? Yes, I have a pattern. I have a pattern of failure and frustration. I knew that before I contacted him. And now I was so steeped in my pattern that I doubted everything I ever believed. I doubted myself.

> **Virgil**: I can help you change your pattern. I have no time to waste with you if you insist on having a problem. Problem thinking will return you to zero again and again and again. In fact, your insistence on having a problem is part of your pattern. If you are not ready or willing to change your pattern it is better if we stop here. It is much better not to start until you are ready to challenge your assumptions and put down what you think you know of success and failure. Do you know the difference between a pattern and a problem?

I didn't know. And, frankly, I was having a hard time knowing why I should care. For a moment I thought about doing what I always do, pretending that I know the answer. I was taught that "not knowing" is a sign of weakness. "Not knowing" meant I was bad at my work. My mentor taught me that I was supposed to know what to do. It's what made a good leader. It was the single-most important quality of a businessperson: know what you are doing. But I was tired, scared and irritated so in defiance, as a challenge, I wrote the truth:

> **Me**: No. I don't know the difference.

> **Virgil**: Good. That is honest and your honesty is a great first step in establishing the new pattern. The old pattern says that you have to know the answer. It says that you have to know what you are doing before you act. It says you have to know where you are going before you take a step. Am I right?

I smelled a trap so I tapped slowly:

> **Me**: Yes. Of course.

> **Virgil**: Good. Then you will understand how important it is for you to take seriously the first step in creating a new pattern. From now on I want you to practice "not knowing."

"What!" I shouted at my screen. I smacked the keys:

Me: What? I don't understand!

Virgil: Precisely. Stop trying to understand. Stop investing in the safety of knowing. The truth is that you don't know. Isn't that what you wrote? You. Don't. Know. This is good news! Growth is never in the direction of knowing; growth is a prerequisite of learning that you do not know. Let yourself learn. Stop protecting yourself from growth and step with honest intention into the truth: you do not know. So, practice the truth. Practice "not knowing."

I typed, "And just how in the hell do I do that?" But then I saw the trap and I erased it. Any "how" question was based on my need to know. I wasn't going to give him the satisfaction of catching me in his trick. So instead I typed:

Me: Okay. Great.

Virgil: Come back to me next week at this time. Through your practice of "not knowing," tell me what you discover about patterns and problems. What's the difference between a pattern and a problem? Why might it be an utter waste of time to think that you have a problem?

3.

I closed my laptop and took a walk. I always walk when I'm confused or frustrated or angry and at the moment I was all three of those things. How was I to practice "not knowing?" It seemed absurd! What did it matter if I saw things as problems and what was the big deal with patterns? I wanted answers to my questions. I wanted to know what to do! I wanted to know why my business failed . . . again.

As I walked I replayed the conversation I'd had at lunch the previous day. I had called my friend Elizabeth. A few years ago she was in the same place I am now: standing amidst the wreckage of her latest business. Like me, she had a long string of projects that *almost* made it. And then, something changed for her. She changed. She was now the CEO of a growing software company. She was very successful. At lunch I confessed my frustration and fear to her. "I need to do something different. Why can't I see what I'm doing wrong?" I nearly shouted.

Elizabeth smiled and folded her hands. "We've had this conversation before," she said. "A couple of times. Do you remember?"

"Yes." I grumbled, stabbing a chunk of potato salad.

"We can have this same conversation again in a few years if you want. Or, you can do what I suggested the last time we had it. Contact Virgil," she said, writing an email address on a slip of paper.

"Who is this guy?" I wanted to know why she was so insistent that I contact him.

"He can help you," she smirked, handing me the slip of paper. Then her expression changed. She got quiet for a moment and said simply, "He helped me. He can help you, too, if you are ready."

"What do you mean, 'if I'm ready?'" I sighed.

"Contact him and find out. Or, do what you always do and we can have lunch again in a year and have this same conversation over again. Are you frustrated enough to change what you are doing?"

I was frustrated enough to contact him. Virgil. And now, as I walked, I was more frustrated than I was before I contacted him. Practice "not knowing!" It made no sense. How was that bit of nonsense supposed to help me with my problem? Oh, right. I almost forgot. According to Virgil, I do not have a problem. I have a pattern. I kicked a pebble and watched it skitter across the street.

I replayed what he wrote:

> **Virgil:** I have no time to waste with you if you insist on having a problem. Problem thinking will return you to zero again and again and again . . . "

As I walked I wrestled with why I should care about the difference between problems and patterns. As if to spite this guy Virgil, I started to look for patterns just to prove that this exercise was pointless. To my surprise, I began seeing patterns everywhere. I noticed the patterns made by bricks in a wall. I saw patterns in the sidewalk. There were patterns in how people mowed their lawns. There was a pattern in my shirt and patterns in the clothes of almost everyone I passed. The trees on the street were planted in a pattern. The houses in my neighborhood were constructed according to a pattern. The more I looked, the more I saw that everything was part of a pattern. In looking for patterns I saw things I'd never seen before, even though I walked these streets everyday. I saw detail and color. More than once I stopped, surprised that I'd never seen this birdhouse or that cluster of flowers. Usually when I walked I was so deep in thought that I didn't see anything. I felt as if I was walking through my neighborhood for the first time. I was seeing it for the first time.

I heard Elizabeth's voice in my head, saying, "Contact Virgil. Or, we can have this conversation over again in a year."

I stood still. I looked all around me. Virgil had written:

> **Virgil:** Your insistence on having a problem is part of your pattern of failure.

Was I acting from a pattern that I could not see? Was I thinking in a pattern that I did not recognize?

I once read that the majority of what we think each day is the same stuff that we thought the day before. We are rolling the exact same thoughts through our heads each day, over and over and over. Only a few thoughts are truly new. What were the patterns of my thinking? What was I rolling through my head each day? Was I walking through my life as blind to my pattern as I was blind to my neighborhood?

It was true that looking for patterns was opening my eyes. I walked slower. This must be what Virgil meant by practicing "not knowing."

4.

When I returned home I found an envelope taped on my front door. Inside there was an index card with this quote:

"Thought is the sculptor who can create the person you want to be."

Henry David Thoreau

5.

It is probably poor form to start a story in the middle, in a moment of high crisis. When a story stalks you through your lifetime you inevitably learn some things about stories; you unwittingly stalk them, too. One of the first things

I learned was that the word "beginning" is arbitrary. An end is always a beginning. A beginning is always an end. What we call a beginning or the middle or an end is really a simple matter of our point of view. It depends on what we see.

When I contacted Virgil I was in crisis.

Another valuable thing I learned about stories is that they unfold according to established patterns. Beginning, middle, and end are a simple pattern. Within this simple pattern is a more complex pattern structure. For instance, in order to grow, the main character has to leave behind everything he knows and go on a journey. That journey can be literal or an inner, metaphoric journey. To leave behind "the known" is part of the pattern that leads to trials, confrontations, and catharsis. It's a pattern. Since each of us is the protagonist in our own story, the pattern is alive and at work in our lives. The trick is to become aware of where you are in the story cycle. Do you need to let go of what you know in order to grow? Are you navigating the trials? What happens once you've experienced catharsis?

Stories never begin with being found. We hear a call. We pursue it blindly and discover that we are lost in the woods. Stories begin when someone, the main character, you, gets lost or is knocked off balance.

This is how I discovered that I was lost in the woods. It went something like this:

I was an organizational consultant and a coach. I had a

business partner, Tim, someone I trusted. I was the creative mind, I was the entrepreneur, the developer of the content and he did the administration and secured contracts. We had a small staff of trainers and facilitators. I was developing a line of products based on the research we had conducted with our clients. There was a book just waiting to be written.

I didn't pay attention to the details of our contracts or the nuts and bolts of our business. That was Tim's realm. Of course, I looked at our budgets, income and expenses, profit and loss statements - and everything always looked in order. We met every week. We talked every day. I prided myself on knowing where we were, knowing where we were going, making sure we stayed on our path and our plan. I thought I knew.

And then one day I arrived at work and Tim had his head on his desk. He was clearly distressed. I asked if he was all right. He looked at me, shook his head. He sat back in his chair and said, "We're bankrupt."

At first it didn't register. "Very funny!" I laughed. He didn't laugh. He averted his eyes. After a moment I said, "But . . . That's not possible."

"We lost our major client. I thought I could get them back so I didn't tell you. They've cancelled the contract. Everything else is . . . the money's already been spent. Now, there's no more coming in. We don't have enough money for rent. We can't pay our phone bill."

"That's not possible," I repeated.

He simply said, "We have to let everyone go."

I remember standing very still, feeling sick to my stomach, not able to comprehend what he was telling me. The only thing I could say was, "It's not possible."

That's the exact moment that the Parcival story took me. It was a funny feeling to be standing there, lost, and to have this story wash into me. Parcival's story was my story and vice versa.

Tim saw it. He asked, "What just happened?" I waved off his question and retreated into my office, closed the door, and sat on the floor while the story that had stalked me all of my life took me and began to reveal its secrets.

You see, like me, Parcival was lost. Like me, he was trying to show off his success.

He had just officially become a knight! In truth, in his nature, he was actually more a fool, more a trickster than knight. But it was a knight he wanted to become and so it was a knight that he became!

After a very auspicious beginning in life, he had been discovered and trained by a master teacher. Now that he'd finally achieved his dream of being knighted, he was lost, riding through the woods, trying to find his way home. He wanted to go home and show his mother that he'd become something great!

Details are important in stories. They reveal pattern. They

are very easy to miss and, once missed, the pattern remains invisible. It is an important detail to know that, at this mid-point where we enter the story, Parcival didn't know his name. His mother had always called him "Dear Son;" she never spoke his name. Just like someone calling me an entrepreneur, or doctor, teacher, lawyer, manager, knight . . . . Parcival was a role. He had no father. He had no siblings. He had no friends. He'd grown up isolated deep in the woods. For all he knew, "Dear Son" was his name.

So he was lost. He was trying to find home. He had been riding for many days and was very tired. The sun was setting when he came upon a wide river and he recognized the place! "Home" was just on the other side of the river. There were no bridges and he knew he'd never be able to cross the river before nightfall. Just then, he spotted a small boat with two old men in it. One old man was fishing and the other guy, a really old guy, was just sitting in the boat. The fisherman saw Parcival and called out to him, saying, "If you seek a place to stay for the night, there is a lovely castle just up the road and you'd be most welcome." Parcival thought, Well, a hot bath, a good meal, and a soft bed to sleep in would be most welcome! He'd find a way to cross the river in the morning. That way, he would be clean and well rested when he arrived home.

Pay attention to this next part of the story. It's the part that washed over me when I stood looking at Tim saying over and over again, "That's not possible."

Parcival thanked the fisherman and, sure enough, about a

mile up the road, was a magnificent castle. He was greeted at the castle gates by lords and ladies, almost as if they were expecting him. They excitedly whisked him into the great hall to meet their king, and much to Parcival's surprise, the king was the fisherman! Only now, instead of wearing the clothes of a poor fisherman, he wore rich robes of the finest silk and luxurious furs. Parcival saw, too, that the king was crippled. The king was in great pain and lay on a couch before a warming fire.

Parcival's mind raced with questions. He'd been taught that it was impolite for a knight to ask his host for explanations. A proper knight must always appear "to know." As a new knight he didn't want to embarrass himself in front of this great king.

The king motioned Parcival to sit beside him, and then he presented Parcival with a beautiful sword. The king looked at Parcival and said, "This sword is destined for you."

If you understood the patterns of story you'd shout at Parcival, "Watch out! Be careful! You do not know what you hold in your hands!" In a good story, when the main character thinks that he knows his destiny, especially when, like me, he has confused himself with a role, the lesson will come with great force, as it did to me. You think you are the recipient of a simple gift, this sword that you hold in your hands. You think you know how to use it. What you don't know is that this gift will use you. What you don't know is so much greater than what you think you know.

Parcival took the sword. He noticed, as he held the king's

gift, that all the lords and ladies stared at him. They were holding their breath waiting to see what Parcival would do. Or say. It seemed that everyone in the castle, from the highest lord to the lowest serving boy was coming into the great hall to see what Parcival would do. Parcival thanked the king for his gift. He desperately wanted to know what the king meant by "destined." He wanted to know why everyone stared at him. But he had been taught it was impolite for a knight to question his host. Accept a gift with gratitude. Be silent. A knight always knows what to do. Ask no questions. Later, he thought, later I will ask my questions of one of the lesser lords.

Just then, a young man came into the hall and a hush fell over the assembly. The young man carried a lance, brilliant white, with a single bead of blood that ran from its tip down the shaft and nearly - but not quite - touched the young man's hand. Every eye watched as the young man processed across the great hall until he exited out the far door, and then all eyes turned and once again stared at Parcival. He was about to panic, when two more men entered the great hall, each carrying a candelabra burning with hundreds of candles. Blinding light filled every corner of the hall. Behind them, a beautiful girl entered. She held in her hands something so brilliant that the candles could not be seen! It was a golden bowl. Its light did not hurt Parcival's eyes. He was transfixed. He had never seen such radiance. Surely this was holy! He watched as they, too, processed across the great hall and vanished out the door on the far side of the hall.

Now his mind burned with questions, questions that he should not ask, questions that he could not ask. He would embarrass himself. He looked to the king and pretended to be cool, the image of a calm, mature, unflappable knight. He pretended that he knew what to do. In truth he was looking for a clue from the king about how to proceed. The king stared back at Parcival, with the same expectation, the same yearning that he saw in the eyes of all the lords and ladies. Parcival nodded politely, quickly pulling his gaze from the king's eyes. To his horror, he watched as the expectation drained from every eye in the room. The stares frosted over and became cold. Parcival quickly looked back to the king but the king had closed his eyes in disappointment. Slowly, the crowd averted their eyes and, without a word, they quietly left Parcival sitting all alone in the great hall.

He'd failed. That was clear. And, like me, he hadn't the slightest idea what had just happened.

6.

It was only a few moments before my next chat with Virgil and I didn't know what to do. I was deciding whether to continue the conversation or just not show up. After my walk the first day, I felt clear about patterns and why I needed to look for them. But, over the course of the week, the more I looked the more confused I became. And now I was more confused than ever.

I saw patterns everywhere. I found patterns in the news cycle, patterns in product marketing, patterns in people's expectations, patterns in television programming, and patterns in politics. When I opened my eyes to look for patterns I noticed that I moved slower and had the feeling that I was capable of seeing what was previously invisible to me. I was seeing the form and not content. I realized I was looking at the movement of things and not the message.

Businesses study customer-buying patterns all the time. The whole point of gathering data is to see patterns. Yet, when I saw patterns I also saw problems to be solved. The patterns in my wallpaper didn't quite match at the seams. I could have solved that problem. My neighborhood coffee-house filled orders in a pattern and there is a bottleneck in their pattern. I could solve that problem in a second! My whole purpose in life was to solve problems and right now I had a problem that I could not solve! According to Virgil, it was a waste of time to think that I had a problem and yet all I could see was my problem. I had a problem! What was the point of denying it?

Was it a waste of time to believe I could solve problems for others, too?

Instead of coming back to Virgil with answers, all I had were more questions. I hated not knowing what to do or say! I felt like I was standing silent before the Sphinx after having a riddle posed to me. A week had passed since Virgil asked me a simple question:

Virgil: What's the difference between a pattern and a problem? Why might it be an utter waste of time to think that you have a problem?"

Now, a week later with my mouth agape and no answers to the riddle, I imagined the Sphinx was about to grin and devour me.

It was abundantly clear that my pattern of thinking was all about problems. And why not? I was taught that an entrepreneur solves problems for people. Problem seeing and problem solving was the organizing principle of my life. When I made pitches to investors the entire format was based on identifying a problem and providing a viable, lucrative solution. I had notebooks filled with ideas for solving problems.

My teacher, my great mentor used to say, "Find the need and fill it." She pounded problem seeking and problem solving into me. "Clarify the problem and you will clarify the solution." I was her gifted student. She used to tell me, "You see the problems that other people overlook." It was true. I could see problems and a million possible solutions. It was also true that I had a string of failed businesses trailing behind me.

I read and re-read the quote I found taped on my door.

"Thought is the sculptor who can create the person you want to be."

What was wrong with my thinking? What was wrong with seeing problems? Seeing problems was my gift and Virgil was telling me that my gift was unusable.

It was time for my appointment. I took a breath. It was time to stand answerless before the Sphinx. I decided I had nothing to lose by keeping the appointment but would delay the conversation about problems for as long as possible. Maybe he'd reveal the answer or better yet, perhaps it just wouldn't come up. I typed:

Me: You there?

Virgil: Hi. Yes. Welcome back. How did it go?

Me: I learned a lot about patterns.

Virgil: Tell me what you discovered.

Me: When I started looking for patterns I saw them everywhere. It was as if everything was connected through some type of pattern. In looking for patterns I started to see things that I'd never before noticed. It was as if the world came into a clearer focus.

Virgil: Good. What else?

Me: Looking for patterns made me move slower. I think that was part of practicing "not knowing," though I'm still not certain that I'm doing what you asked.

Virgil: Lol! And in this way, for now, your uncertainty is a great way of practicing "not knowing."

I hated that. In my present circumstance there was nothing great about uncertainty. I ignored him and wrote:

Me: I realized that I think in patterns. I think the same stuff over and over. This is a puzzle: the act of looking for patterns opened my eyes. So, patterns reveal. And yet, later, when I became aware of the patterns of my thinking, I recognized that those patterns were like ruts or grooves. It's as if I am playing the same song over and over again so no other music can come in. My thinking pattern, my rut, prevents me from seeing. So patterns also obscure. Make sense?

Virgil: Yes. It must seem like a paradox to you. Think of the song or rut as a story that you tell yourself. Your thoughts, literally, are a story that you tell yourself about yourself and the world; the more you tell this story the deeper the rut you create. So, a good question to ask is: what is the story that you want to tell? Are you creating the pattern that you desire to create? We will return to this many times. This is important: the story is not happening to you; you are telling it. The story can only control you if you are not aware that you are telling it.

Me: Can you say more?

Virgil: We literally 'story' ourselves. We are hard-wired for story. What we think is a narrative; this pattern (song) that rolls through your mind everyday is a story that you tell. You tell it. It defines what you see and what you do not see. What you think is literally what you see.

There was a pause. That was a lot for me to take in. When I didn't respond, he continued:

Virgil: So, what you think is nothing more than a story; it's an interpretation. You move through your day seeing what you think instead of what is there. You are not seeing the world; you are seeing your interpretation of the world. You are seeing from your rut and your rut is a pattern. So, your patterns of thinking, your rut, can obscure what you see. Make sense?

Me: Yes. I guess ;-) So, when I started looking for patterns outside of me, I . . . stopped seeing from within my rut? I stopped assuming that I knew what I was seeing. So, I was capable of discovering new patterns and connections?

Virgil: Yes, something like that. You said that when you looked for patterns you slowed down and felt that you could see. I would say it this way: you stopped moving *through* your world and for a brief period you were actually *in* your world. For a brief period you were no longer lost in thought but present with what was right in front of you. You suspended what you think you know so you started to see again. You were curious. To be curious is synonymous with "not knowing."

Me: Okay . . .

Virgil: Humor me and entertain this notion: your thought, your story, is not passive. It is a creative act. What you think IS what you see.

> Most of the time people create what they see
> based on their rut. They see what they expect
> to see. To practice curiosity is to suspend the
> assumption of knowing. To practice curiosity
> requires us to step out of the rut. Stop assum-
> ing that you know and you gain the capacity
> to see beyond what you think."

A glimmer of light pierced the dark recesses of my mind.
Suddenly I was back in front of the Sphinx and I could see
the answer to the riddle. It was so clear! I typed:

> **Me**: Wait! Is this why I need to distinguish
> between problems and patterns? If I tell myself
> that I have a problem to solve, I am telling a
> certain kind of story. If I tell myself that I have
> a pattern to change, I am telling an entirely
> different kind of story. Is that true?

> **Virgil**: Yes. It sounds too simple, doesn't it?
> A problem is a story. It is a lens that filters
> your sight. A problem does not exist unless
> you insist that it is there. You say that you are
> an entrepreneur. How many great products
> and services were the results of an accident in
> the lab? How many innovations were missed
> because the 'solution' did not fit the 'problem'
> as identified? A problem is a rut that separates
> you from possibilities. On the other hand, a

pattern connects you to possibilities. See the pattern, not the problem.

Me: But, how does this help me in my business?

Virgil: The pattern or story you tell will determine the possibilities you see or don't see. The story you tell will determine the actions you see or do not see. For instance, you said that once you started looking you saw patterns everywhere. You saw connectivity; everything seemed part of a greater pattern.

Me: Yes. It was a discovery. It was wonderful.

Virgil: What did that discovery lead you to do?

Me: Well, I slowed down. I looked. I saw things . . . I started seeing a bigger context. I saw relationships between things. I saw how things were shaped . . . I saw how things could be improved. I was seeing through different eyes.

Virgil: That would seem to be an important skill for an entrepreneur, don't you agree?

What potential would become visible to you
if you flipped from seeing problems to seeing
patterns?

After our chat I received an email from Virgil with this:

**The First Recognition: You do not have a problem.
You have a pattern.**

Study: Learn to distinguish between a problem and
a pattern. Study patterns as distinct from problems.
Innovators do not solve problems, they pursue, they
reveal, they discover, they integrate and establish
new patterns. Study your patterns.

Action: Practice "Not Knowing." Get curious. Take
steps because you don't know what will happen. Do
things in a different order; go home by a different
route. Get lost on purpose.

Exercise: 1) Look for patterns all around you; look
inside and outside of you. What are the patterns you
see in others? What are your patterns? 2) Make a list
of all the things you pretend to know. Why do you
need to pretend? What do you get from pretending
to know? How does your need to pretend reveal your
patterns?

Recognition 2: Your language matters

7.

It's a common characteristic of stories that the main character tries again and again to solve a new problem but he doesn't recognize that he is operating from old information. And then, one day, he finally sees that the old information is not useful. He has to stop and admit to himself that he doesn't know what to do. All that he knows for certain is that he doesn't know what to do. It's a paradox. This is a powerful and necessary step in the progress of the story. It's the point in every story and every life when the real seeking begins. It is the point that seeing becomes possible.

Once, years ago, when I was in college I did some work in alternative schools. These "alternative schools" were safety nets for kids who had dropped out, the schools for kids who the system had failed. What I appreciated most about the alternative schools was that the teachers would try anything to reignite the flame of curiosity in a student. The traditional path had snuffed the kid's curiosity. The kids equated learning with pain. The teachers in the alternative schools never knew where they were going. They never had an answer. They knew that the traditional path didn't work; they were certain that they didn't know what to do. In the absence of a path, they would try anything. I admired them. More than once I was astounded by their ingenuity.

I'd completely forgotten about my experiences in the alternative schools until Virgil asked me to practice "not knowing." After our initial chat I was confused and felt he was being purposefully obscure. What does it mean to practice "not knowing?" It seemed crazy. And then he suggested that practicing curiosity was the same thing as "not knowing." The light bulb turned on.

After our latest chat I took another walk. I was pissed again. Not right away - everything he wrote made sense. And then I started thinking about it and the more I thought about it the angrier I became. I'm starting to think that being pissed is one of my patterns. I had to process what we discussed. I had to clear my head. I wanted coffee.

Virgil was challenging the foundations of everything I'd been taught and led to believe. As I walked I felt stupid and also more than a bit impatient. I wanted to know how to whip up my curiosity. There must be a recipe, a few simple steps. Besides, I identified myself as someone who is curious in the world. I am a risk taker. He was implying that I was not who I thought I was. He was implying that my world was built on old information and the reason my business failed was merely a matter of a pattern of applying old information to a new . . . dare I say, "problem."

And during our chat, just as happened before, as I was getting frustrated because I wanted a concrete answer from him, because I wanted to know what to do, his response was the opposite of what I expected. His answer was to embrace the truth which was that I did not know where I was going. I was lost and his suggestion was to embrace rather than fight the truth that I did not know what to do. He'd written:

> **Virgil**: Stand firmly in not knowing and see what's there. Why do you insist on rushing past your truth?

Needless to say, when I read that, I shouted at my screen, "This is crazy!" while at the same time, for some reason, I typed that I agreed to try his suggestion. So, I had to take a walk.

While I was walking off my irritation, grumbling that this whole thing was a waste of time and I'd have been better off to have never contacted the mysterious Virgil and his insistence that I practice "not knowing," I remembered the alternative schools. Those teachers were more innovative, more creative and alive than anyone I knew in business school.

It occurred to me as once again I stood still in the middle of my street, that those teachers were vital and innovative *because* they were certain that they didn't know what to do. Virgil was asking me to be like the teachers I so admired.

8.

I set down my stuff at my usual table at the coffeehouse and went to the counter and ordered a mocha. When I returned to my table I found this quote typed into the notes on my iPad:

"One must be leery of words because words turn into cages."

Viola Spolin

9.

We tell our stories with words. That would seem obvious but it's not. We tell the stories of our lives with our words. That would seem obvious, too, but it is not. Once, I went to a lecture given by a man who was born into a tribal community in South America. He said something that hit me like a ton of bricks: "You think putting a spell on someone is magic! You misunderstand the word 'spell.' A 'spell' is not mystical or hocus-pocus! No! That is to misunderstand the power of words! In my culture we understand that to tell a little girl that she is fat is to spell her forever. This is not hocus-pocus. This is the power of your words."

When Tim said, "We're bankrupt," his words spelled me. I have no memory of leaving the office after he uttered those words. It's as if I fell into a time warp. "We're bankrupt." The words I began using against myself went something like this: You are a loser. You are a failure. Powerful words, indeed! I began weaving a nasty spell on myself.

Much of Parcival's story is about the labels we put on our experiences. I learned from the story about the power of a single word.

After Parcival's failure, he had no memory of leaving the great hall.

Parcival knew that he'd failed but had no idea how or why. Like me, he'd achieved his dream and then things went terribly wrong. He awoke the next morning in a strange bed.

Although groggy and disoriented, he felt well fed. He was clean, but he had no memory of eating or taking a bath. Upon rising he was surprised to find that there was no one in the castle. Everyone was gone, the king, the lords, the ladies, the servants, the cooks and pages. He'd planned to ask someone about the procession, about the lance, the blood and the brilliant golden bowl. He called out, wandering through the halls but his voice echoed off the stone walls. The castle was completely deserted.

He thought that maybe he had dreamed the whole affair but there he was in the castle. He held the sword that the Fisher King had given him. It was real. Confused, he strapped on his armor, secured the new sword, mounted his horse, and with a heavy heart he rode out of the castle. He crossed the open drawbridge and just as his horse stepped off the bridge onto the land, the drawbridge rose quite suddenly, goosed his poor horse, and closed behind him with a bang! Parcival turned to see what had happened, and the castle was gone! It had vanished. There was no moat, no drawbridge, and no castle.

He stared across an empty meadow into a dense forest. Now he was frightened. His horse reeled and when he finally brought it under control, he saw stepping out of the forest the young woman who'd carried the golden bowl. He was frozen by her stare. She said nothing, only glowered at him for a long time. And without really knowing why, Parcival dropped his head in shame.

"Your name is Parcival," she called to him, and he knew it was true. "You will be forever known as Parcival the Unfortunate. Your sword, the king's gift, will fail when you need it most just as you failed us when we most needed you."

Parcival took a sharp breath to stop his hot tears. He was angry and raised his eyes to meet hers. He wanted to ask her what had happened, what was going on, who was she, and how did she know his name? But, just like the castle, she had vanished.

She had named him and her words were powerful.

Parcival sat on his horse staring into the forest for a long time. He didn't know what to do. Finally, he decided that before going home he must ride quickly to King Arthur's court and present himself to Arthur, his King. Perhaps the Knights of the Round Table could help him understand what had just happened to him. More important, perhaps they could tell him what he should do.

10.

Parcival rode to Camelot seeking answers. I had rushed to Elizabeth hoping to find answers and she goaded me into contacting Virgil. I wanted Virgil to tell me what I should do. I wanted him to fix me or tell me how to become successful. Instead of answers I had more questions.

I confess I was slightly unhinged in the coffeehouse when I found the quote typed into my iPad.

"One must be leery of words because words turn into cages."

Who would do that? Was it Virgil? How did he do it without my seeing it? And why did he leave that specific quote for me?

Words are more powerful than we know. I think this is at least part of what Virgil is trying to get me to see. If I put a label on it, that is what I will see. So far, that's the crux of his message to me.

I remember reading the part in the Bible when Adam gives names to everything. It was as an act of ritual claiming.

Give it a name and that's how it will be seen. I realized that naming an experience good or bad, right or wrong, best or worst is the same thing - a form of claiming. I name my experiences like Adam named the animals! If I name it then that is what I see. When I label my business a failure, when I call myself a failure, then that is what I am and that's all I will ever see!

Now I could understand why Virgil was so adamant to make me distinguish between having a problem and work-ing on a pattern. Now I understood the power behind his lesson. I was starting to fully grasp why I needed to practice "not knowing." With "knowing" comes prescribed labels. With "not knowing" the labeling process is interrupted. Then, at least, the naming is conscious.

It is a matter of order. "To know" is to place a label on an experience before having the experience. To "not know" is to reverse the order: the labels follow the experience. Virgil would call this reversal of order a flip.

Reading the story of Parcival as a boy, I couldn't imagine not knowing my name. I was intrigued by the part in the story when the woman comes out of the forest and tells Parcival his name. In a single stroke, in one simple word, she names him and in his mind he transforms from being a generic role, "Dear Son," to someone specific with a name, "Parcival." His whole world turned on one simple word. And then, BAM! Before he could fully inhabit his new name she tacked on a label: "the Unfortunate." He would forever see his life through the eyes of that simple phrase, the Unfortunate.

When my business collapsed my friends said things like, "It's a stroke of bad luck!" or "Not your fault!" or "The next one will be the charm." It was exactly the same stuff they told me the last time my business failed. And, I believed it! It was a stroke of bad luck. It wasn't my fault. There is a charm out there somewhere and if I keep looking I will find it. So, my success was dependent upon a charm and had nothing to do with my hard work. BAM! Suddenly I, too, was "the Unfortunate."

Perhaps Virgil was not delusional after all. When I started listening to *how* I named my story I saw that I was the one who was delusional. Maybe there was a layer beneath problems and patterns that he was trying to get me to see.

I pulled up our last chat sequence and read it. My mouth dropped open when I read what I'd written about looking for patterns:

> **Me:** . . . I saw relationships between things. I saw how things were shaped . . . . I saw how things could be improved. I was seeing through different eyes.

Instead of trying to solve for a problem, what if I had eyes that could see how things were patterned so I could clearly see how they might be improved?

I scribbled this note on the yellow pad next to my computer:

Words matter. A problem exists like an island in isolation. It is mechanistic thinking. Call it a problem and you will assume that you know a solution: cause and effect - and all you can do is fix or solve. There is an end. A pattern reveals connections. It is dynamic and reveals structure, composition, and design. Call it a pattern and you will assume that you don't know because there is no end to the improvements you can see - it extends into the future beyond the vanishing point. The best you can do is walk toward it.

11.

Stories and story cycles are patterns. There are endless story formulas out there to describe what makes a story work. One of my favorite definitions of story comes from Robert Olen Butler. He writes that a story happens when a yearning meets an obstacle.

This is a simple pattern and the result is energy! Nothing creates movement toward fulfillment than a yearning meeting an obstacle.

I had a revelation after scribbling my note. I wanted Virgil to tell me how to do it so it would be easy. I wanted him to tell me the answer. My assumption was that an answer exists and I just can't see it. That is another form of problem thinking. What if there are multiple answers? What if there are no answers but more and more steps? Isn't that a great description of business in the 21st century? If I lived in the

19th century it might be appropriate to problem solve. The world I inhabit moves too fast. Moore's Law is in play. Ambiguity and rapid change are the constants. That is why it is an imperative that I recognize that I have patterns not problems. Problem solving is like looking at the ground while the world passes by; pattern recognition demands that you keep your head up and eyes open.

The name I give things either opens my eyes or blinds me to what's possible. My language matters!

I sent an email to Virgil telling him of my insight and he responded that I'd stumbled into the second recognition: language matters. He congratulated me and then asked me this question:

> **Virgil:** Are you ready to leave behind all that
> you know?

I wrinkled my nose at the words on the screen. I knew exactly what he was asking of me and didn't like what it implied.

The Second Recognition: Your language matters

Study: Turn your practice of "not knowing" back on yourself. Listen to the words you use to tell your story. How often do you say "can't" or "have to?" Do you often use "should?" Study the words you use to tell your story.

Action: Language matters so play with changing words or phrases like "can't" or "have to" into "choose" or "choose not to." Use the language of choice for a week. How does your story change? How does your seeing change?

Exercise: Eavesdrop. Listen to the language of other people. Pay attention to their conversations as if they were stories being created. What words matter in how people story themselves?

Recognition 3: You are telling yourself a story

12.

It is one thing to name yourself. It is another to have others name you. My former employees named me. They called me "liar." I'd made big promises that I could not keep. They said, "You knew it was collapsing! You had to know and lied to us." My investors labeled me, too. The names they gave me were things like "reckless," "irresponsible," and "ridiculous."

Parcival was given a label, too: The Unfortunate. After the woman gave Parcival his name and thus labeled him, he decided that he must ride quickly to Arthur's court and present himself to his King. Perhaps the Knights of the Round Table could help him understand what had just happened. He wanted answers! It was not far. After a few days of hard riding he entered the gates of Camelot. The knights were waiting for him. They immediately embraced him as a brother knight. They knew his name: "Parcival of Wales," they called him. They welcomed him home to Camelot. They whisked him away to the great hall to see King Arthur.

But before he could tell the knights what had happened in the disappearing castle, and before he could ask them what it all meant, there was a commotion in the great hall. The lords and ladies gasped. The knights surrounding Parcival were repulsed and parted as they caught sight of a hideous hag (in the story she is known as the Loathly Damsel - a role, not a name). She rode an ass which clopped slowly through the crowd and stopped directly in front of Parcival.

The woman was broken and hunchbacked. Her eyes were yellow and she had a nose like a rat. Her teeth were black and rotted and she had a beard like a goat. She pointed a gnarled finger at Parcival and looked to the assembled knights, lords and ladies. She cried, "He, he . . . this one has brought the land to waste! Because of this one, this coward, many knights will die, many ladies will be widowed and many children orphaned. Many will starve!"

And then she told them of Parcival's failure to seize his opportunity at the Grail Castle. He failed to speak his truth. And, because he'd failed, the land would be laid to waste and the Fisher King would remain in agony. She sneered at Parcival and then she spat, and without another word, she turned her mount and they slowly clopped away.

All were stunned. And, for the second time, Parcival found that every eye in the court turned to look at him, and then they, too, averted their eyes and slowly left him standing all alone in the great hall.

Like Parcival, I took the names others called me and added them to the names I called myself. It made for a dark and shameful story. Like Parcival, I, too, accepted that I was responsible for the wasteland. I had no idea what went wrong or why. I felt that I somehow deserved these names so I folded them into my now dark story.

13.

When I was a little kid I had a paper route. Every morning I got up before the sun. I folded and banded the papers. I stuffed them in a big canvas shoulder bag and walked the neighborhood putting newspapers on porches. I never threw the papers on the porches. I placed them. Placing the papers on the porches was my innovation. Some of my friends had routes and their parents drove them through the neighborhood. They tossed the papers from the car, sometimes hitting the porch and sometimes not. Even then

I had an expectation; there was a better way and I could find it. It was a kind of personal code of honor: improve upon what's already there.

When I went door-to-door collecting money for the paper, I asked my customers' where exactly would they like their papers placed on the porch? Would they like them tucked between the screen and the front door? I asked if there was a good time of day for me to collect the money so that I didn't interrupt their dinner? Was there a better day of the week to collect? They were amused, surprised, and supportive - and I took note that they always had an answer. They had a preference. Knowing their preferences was my innovation. I collected my data and made customer preference charts. I delivered my papers and collected my money according to my customers' preferences. I learned their names.

My route flourished. Soon I had to loop back home to refill my bag because I couldn't carry all the papers in one load. I had to get up earlier and earlier because it took longer to fold, band and walk the route with my growing customer base. People called the newspaper office to compliment my delivery service. The newspaper printed a small story about me. The reporter doing the story asked me how I came up with my ideas and I remember not having an answer for the question. I thought everyone was trying to improve the way things were done. It was the first time that I realized I was not like the others. Improving upon things was natural to me. It was how I looked at the world and it was unique.

The man in charge of paper deliveries gave me an award. I was held up to the other delivery boys as an example of how to do a good job. I didn't really care about the award; I knew it was made-up and meant to be an incentive for the other delivery boys. What excited me was realizing that I had an advantage and my advantage was not in how I did my work, the doing came second. My advantage was in how I saw my work. My friends thought delivering papers was a task. I knew it was a business. I don't know how I knew but I already understood that there was a vast difference between doing a task and creating a business. I knew my business was about knowing my customers' preferences. I knew my business was about standing in other people's shoes and seeing what might make life easier for them; it only looked like I was delivering newspapers.

I was telling myself a much different story than all of the other delivery boys.

14.

When I first contacted Virgil he wrote:

> **Virgil:** You don't know what you don't know.

He's trying to help me see what is right in front of me but I do not see.

This morning I made a list of all the things I did right in my business. I remembered a meeting I had several months ago with a potential client. I realized there was an important flip side to Virgil's statement: you don't know what you don't know. The flip side is this: you don't know what you *DO* know. Some things are so natural to me. I see things and assume that everyone can see it, too. They don't. I am constantly surprised when something so clear to me is invisible to someone else.

The client came to me because she was certain that her situation was impossible. She'd just been appointed as the director of a student services center at a university. The previous director was a bully and the culture of the center was toxic. My client wanted to change the culture of the center. She hired consultants who brought her models for building better teams; she held weekly meetings to give her staff the opportunity to share their thoughts; she had an open door policy so her staff would know that she was accessible. But, in her words, "Nothing seems to work."

It seemed so obvious to me.

"How long have you been the director?" I asked.

"Three months already!" she replied.

"How long was the previous director at the center?"

"Six years. He was awful. He was terribly abusive," she said.

"Are your staff members machines or humans?" I asked and she wrinkled her brow. I added, "I'm not being flip. I'm asking you a serious question."

She sat for a moment before responding. "You mean this is

going to take time."

"Have you ever been hurt in a relationship?"

"Of course." She was wary of this line of questioning.

"How long did it take before you trusted the next person who came into your life?" I asked and she began to laugh.

"You mean they've been burned and I'm the new girl-friend," she smiled.

"Yes. Imagine for a moment that you are the new girlfriend and you're dealing with someone who's been burned badly; what would you do?"

"It's going to take time, isn't it?" She closed her eyes and nodded her head, continuing, "And I need to help them learn that I am safe. They need to take little steps for a while. They need to trust that I'm not anything like the former director. A little wooing is in order. A little kindness would help. This is not a problem to fix, it's a new relationship to develop."

"Exactly." I smiled.

She stood, shook my hand and said, "It's so simple when I look at it like that."

15.

I don't know what I don't know. And, I don't know what I do know. I'm practicing not knowing. I'm telling myself,

"Be curious." And, it is hard because all I want right now is to know. I want an answer. I want a prescription. I want to see where I'm going. I want to know what to do.

And then I found an envelope tucked into my shoulder bag. I opened the envelope and found this quote written on stationary from the Holiday Inn Express in Hastings, Nebraska:

"People take on the shapes of the songs and the stories that surround them, especially if they don't have their own song."

Neil Gaiman

16.

Children don't know what they can and can't do so they imagine themselves capable of all things; it's "not knowing" that makes all things possible. Parcival's story begins with the freedom of a child's mind and the uninhibited action that comes from not knowing. Reclaiming this freedom in adulthood is the point of many stories. It is essential to the entrepreneurial mindset.

The beginning of the story goes something like this: the first time Parcival rode into Arthur's court he was just leaving his boyhood behind and he was not yet a man. Everyone stared at him that time, too. Worse, they laughed at him. It was just about lunchtime. All the knights were on the parade grounds, exercising, practicing their skills, jousting and fencing. Onto the grounds rode this young lout, the boy Parcival, astride a mule. He was engulfed in a shabby suit of clothes, like baggy pajamas with big broad horizontal stripes. He wore reeds knit together and meant to be a breastplate and he carried a stick that he wielded like a sword. On his head he wore slates of wooden shingles that he had fashioned into a crude helmet. He was proud of his armor. It's what knights wear, he thought.

As he dismounted, his mule brayed and bucked, and knocked him down. He dusted himself off and announced to the wide-eyed gathering that, "I am here to become a knight of the round table and offer my services to the great King Arthur."

He bowed low and his hat fell off. Everyone roared with laughter.

Arthur was enjoying this joke so he played along. Arthur was certain that one of his knights had set this up. So, in mock seriousness, Arthur asked the boy-knight to announce his name to the assembled host. Remember, Parcival didn't know his name. His mother had never told him his name. He announced dramatically, "I am called Dear Son." He struck a pose like he imagined a knight might strike at such a moment and stepped on the rough edge of his baggy trousers which dropped to his knees. Arthur howled! The other knights laughed so hard they had to sit down. Some fell to their knees and pounded the ground. This was a good joke! With tears running into his beard Arthur turned to his knights and through his laughter said,

"I don't know which one of you louts set this up, but I'll get you. I'll get you back!" He wiped the laughter from his eyes, slapped Parcival on the back and thanked him for his good jest. Then he turned to the knights and said, "Let's go eat!" The knights roared and laughed and stampeded into the great hall.

They left Parcival standing all alone, his trousers around his ankles and his shingle hat broken on the ground. He didn't understand what just happened.

I didn't catch it until now that Parcival is left standing alone in shame three times in the story: once at the Grail Castle, once in the great hall of Camelot, and this time, the first time on the parade grounds with his pants down around his ankles. This time, the first time, he does something completely different. He does not acknowledge the shame. He does not participate. He does not seek to understand what he did wrong because he doesn't see anything wrong. He stays on his intention. It's beautiful.

Parcival had grown up deep in the forest. He never knew his father. He never even knew he had a father. He never knew that he had an older brother. Both his father and his brother had been great knights in Arthur's court and both had been killed in the wars to unite the kingdom. Parcival's mother took her infant son, swearing that he would never know about the court or wars or knights or men, and fled deep into the forest. She raised her son ignorant of all worldly matters. And so Parcival grew into a handsome, naive, impulsive, very talkative - some would say boorish

- young man. He was not schooled in numbers or letters or even manners for that matter. He knew nothing of girls and, except for his mother, he knew nothing of other people. This is the ideal upbringing for a trickster - a great fool. He was a nature boy; that is, he acted purely, with no inhibition, from his nature. He did not know what he did not know.

At the beginning of his story Parcival had no obstacles and no yearnings. He was a wild child living in the moment. So, you can imagine Parcival's surprise when, one day, running through the woods, howling like a wolf, he ran smack into five knights. Literally. He thought they were gods. They sat high on their warhorses, shiny and grand in their armor. They asked him to get off his knees, asked him to please stop bowing; it was embarrassing to them. They told him they were Knights of the Round Table and served the great King Arthur. They were not gods nor were they angels. The castle where they lived, called Cam-A-Lot, was just a few days ride over that way. They thought the boy was touched because, after he got off his knees, he asked an endless stream of questions without waiting for a single reply. They had to ride fast to get away from him. "We have an appointment," one of them lied, "must be getting on!" and they galloped away.

Something awoke inside Parcival that day. He felt something new. He swore he would become a knight of the Round Table - even though he had no idea what that meant. It was his destiny. He knew it!

Parcival left the forest, he left his mother (she was devastated), he fashioned clothes that he thought a knight would wear, grabbed the closest thing to a horse that he could find and rode into the court. That's how he came to be standing alone on the parade grounds of Camelot with his pants down around his ankles and his shingle-hat broken on the ground.

He felt no shame. He experienced no inhibition. He pulled up his pants, caught his mule, mounted and rode straight into the great hall where all the knights were eating lunch. He didn't know any better. He didn't know this was considered at court to be a declaration of war. How could he have known? His mule crashed through the massive wooden doors of the great hall. The knights leapt to their feet, swords drawn as Parcival astride his mule rode straight toward the king. Only Arthur's signal kept the knights from slicing and dicing the boy to death.

Parcival, sitting high atop his mule, stared straight at the king and said, "I demand to be made a knight of a round table." As you can imagine, the blood of rage rushed into Arthur's face. No one, not even a clown, demanded anything from the king.

Parcival, not knowing any better, not aware of any shame or reason why he shouldn't ask for what he wanted, stared back at the now angry king and said, "Well? How do I do this?"

17.

Stories often deal with the collision that arises when learned patterns blind us to our natural impulses. Living according to what we "should do" or "should think" inevitably collides with what we desire to do and this provides a hot crucible for growth. When Virgil asked me to practice "not knowing" he was poking a hole in my story of "should do" so that I might once again hear what I intuitively knew to be true. Stories show us how to get out of our own way. As Virgil recently wrote:

> **Virgil**: You are at one time the source of your yearning and your greatest obstacle. What you think that you should do IS the obstacle to your desire.

In my latest chat with Virgil I told him of my revelations about 'not knowing what I DO know,' about my memory of my client, and how I convinced her that she didn't need me and could do the work by herself. I wrote:

> **Me**: At the time I really needed the money. I needed the business! And I spent that morning convincing a potential client that she didn't need me. It's the story of my life!

He responded:

> **Virgil:** Oh, you are dangerously close to the third recognition.

I decided I needed to stop being careful with how I said things to Virgil. I'd just learned that my language mattered so I might as well write what I was thinking:

> **Me:** Well, maybe you should tell me before I trip over something and hurt myself. You must have an answer or two in there somewhere.

> **Virgil:** I'm woefully low on answers but I do have a question for you: What did you mean when you wrote: It's the story of my life?

> **Me:** I don't know. It was just a phrase, an attempt at humor.

> **Virgil:** What if it's not just a phrase?

> **Me:** You mean that convincing people that they don't need my services is the story of my life? That is why my business crashed?

> **Virgil:** No. I'm not inferring, interpreting or implying anything. You used this phrase: It is the story of my life. I'm asking you to consider that this is more than a flippant phrase. Are you aware of the story of your life?

I was getting angry again. And, I was beginning to recognize that my anger was a pattern that flared when I felt lost. I get angry when I am driving and miss my turn or can't find where I'm going. I wanted a map. I wanted Virgil to be my personal GPS and tell me where to go. Where were we going with this? Sometimes I can't help my sarcasm:

> **Me**: You mean I only get one story!

> **Virgil**: Your story is not something you get. Remember, your language matters. Choose your words more carefully and you might see the third recognition before you trip over it. Connect the dots. Tripping over it will not hurt you . . . it's the choice to be blind that causes your pain.

18.

I sat staring at my screen for several minutes after he signed off. I felt admonished for my sarcasm, as though he'd sent me to bed with no supper. What was the big deal?

If I embrace the notion that my language matters then his point was obvious wasn't it? If my story was not something I get then it must be something I tell. Or give?

It was starting to dawn on me that there was a deeper pattern that he was trying to get me to see. There was a good reason why he had no patience for my sarcasm. When I used the words "I only get one story" I allow myself to believe that someone else gives me my story. If someone else gives me my story then I am never responsible for what happens. I am not to blame. On the other hand, when I switch a single word and say, "I only tell one story" then no one else is to blame. No one else is responsible for my story.

I can choose to be a victim. Or I can choose to be a creator. The difference is the story I tell.

The deeper pattern was one of responsibility. The deeper pattern was about ownership. It is why he asked me to begin by discerning between problems and patterns. Problems happen to me; patterns are something I create. I can change the pattern.

I learned that what I name things either opens my eyes or blinds me to what's possible - and the only difference is the language I choose. I choose it. It doesn't happen to me. My language matters because it defines the story I tell.

So, my story is not given to me. I am telling myself a story. I used the phrase, "The story of my life" to imply that I have an uncontrollable pattern and my pattern is to miss business opportunities. Now, I see the phrase in a different way: The story of my life is a story that I tell.

I did not miss an opportunity with the director of the student services center. I helped her see what she could not see. I did for her what Virgil was doing for me. I didn't drop answers on her or provide clever and expensive yet unnecessary solutions. I simply asked her a question. I am in a service industry and I served her need, not my need.

19.

I chatted with Virgil later that night and told him of my insights about the story of my life. I told him how my perception flipped and I recognized that my life story is a story I tell.

> **Virgil:** Yes. The third recognition is, in fact, just that simple: you are telling yourself a story. It is probably too early but I will plant this seed now: great change is never in the big complicated interventions. It is always found in the simple, the small steps. The actions we need to take are rarely difficult; the story we wrap around the necessary actions make them seem harder than they are.

He continued:

> **Virgil:** Before we move on, it is important to put together the recognitions so far: You don't have a problem; you have a pattern. See the patterns in your life. One of the most important patterns you need to see is your

word choice. Your words matter because they are the building blocks of the story you tell. Are you telling a story of "things happening to you," or are you telling a story of, "I make things happen." Entrepreneurs tell the latter story. The story you tell is revealed through the patterns of your life. Do you see? It is a loop.

Me: Yes. I see that now.

Virgil: You've already acknowledged that you don't know the story that you tell yourself. You are blind to it. Assume that you do not know so you can begin to hear the story. Begin by listening to the language you use in telling your story. What are the patterns of language you use? What do those patterns reveal about the story you tell?

Entrepreneurs and artists have many things in common. Most significantly, they are telling themselves an entirely different story than most people tell so they see a world that is different than most people see. Seeing relationships and bigger contexts, seeing trends and patterns is sometimes called foresight. That would seem to be another important skill for an entrepreneur, wouldn't you agree?

The Third Recognition: You are telling yourself a story

Study: Continue to turn your curiosity onto yourself: study the story you tell. Are you telling the story of "things happen to you?" or are you telling the story of, "I make things happen?"

Action: Sometimes hurricanes come and blow your house away. This is called circumstance. You may have no power over your circumstance but you have infinite choice over how you are within your circumstance. This is called story. Draw a line down the middle of a sheet of paper. At the top, on one side, write "circumstance." On the other side write, "story." Consider any challenge that you currently face: what is circumstance (what is out of your control) and what is story (how you interpret your circumstance).

Exercise: Listen to every conversation, meeting, interaction, and engagement as if it was a story being created. Develop the ears to hear the two types of story: 1) Things happen to me, and 2) I make things happen.

Cycle Two: Story

Recognition 4: You locate yourself within your story

20.

I was late for a meeting and raced out to my car, spilling my coffee as I went. I found a greeting card tucked into my windshield wiper. The image on the card was a photograph of kids playing in a refugee camp. This quote was written inside:

"Experience is not what happens to you; it's what you do with what happens to you." Aldous Huxley

Someone had to be watching me. I tried to be subtle and see if I could catch them spying on me. There was no one else on the street. No one was peeking between bushes. There wasn't a suspicious van parked on the street. I wondered if there was a camera that I couldn't see. Then I felt silly about the story I was telling and started to laugh.

21.

In our next chat Virgil wrote:

> **Virgil:** There are nine recognitions, three loops of three recognitions each. You've closed the first loop. It is called "patterns." The next three recognitions form a loop that we'll call "story." This doesn't mean that you leave patterns behind. Continue your practice of "not knowing," seek to see patterns, choose your language, and always be aware that you are telling yourself a story.

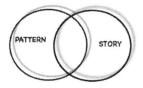

Me: Is there a deeper reason for talking about business through the lens of story? I understand it for my personal growth. Why is it important for the success of my business?

Virgil: The idea that they are separate things is an old world notion. Compartmentalization, the idea that you can separate your emotions from your work, your ethics from your actions, your values from your interests, belongs to the age of the iron horse. You are living in the greatest era of personal and professional revolution since Gutenberg invented the printing press. This is the era of connectivity, not component parts. Your story is living, dynamic, and fluid. How you conduct yourself in life is how you do business. Entrepreneurship, like artistry, is not about what you do; it is about how you orient yourself within your life.

Me: You gave me an exercise after the last recognition- to distinguish between my circumstance and how I am within my circumstance. Is this what you mean about orienting?

Virgil: Partially. Making the distinction between your circumstance and who you are within your circumstance is very important.

Most people confuse the two: they think they
are their circumstance. For instance, your business failed and so you started calling yourself
a failure. You confused yourself with your circumstance. Circumstance: your business failed.
Story: I am a failure. Another possible story: I
learn from my experiences. It is important for
you to continue to make this distinction. This
is only one aspect of orienting yourself in your
life.

He continued:

Virgil: Since we are discussing orienting to
yourself within your life, I want to give you
two more practices to add to your practice
of "not knowing." Most people are incapable
of learning because they are too invested in
judging themselves. (Note: judging others is
the same thing as judging yourself. We'll work
with this more later but for now assume that
judgment in any form impedes learning.) When
you contacted me you were incapable of learning because you were so full of self-judgment.
Just as patterns and problems are dance part-
ners, so, too, are learning and judgment. The
goal is to help you see opportunity wherever
you look. To have the eyes to see opportunity
you must first be capable of learning at every

moment. To develop this capability, you need two additional practices:

1) Have experiences first and make meaning second. This is actually how your brain works. You have experiences, feel sensation, and then you make meaning of the experience. This process of meaning making is what I call story. Children have no problem with this practice. They live to try things and then they make sense of what they just experienced. Adults flip it over and therefore block themselves: they think they need to know before they act. Do you see why practicing "not knowing" is so vital? So, practice what every child knows: have the experience first (practice not know- ing), ACT . . . and then make meaning from what you experience.

2) Judgment is nothing more than a signal that you've left your comfort zone. It is a siren that says, "You've come to an edge!" For adults, all learning happens at the edges - because we've learned that it is uncomfortable to "not know." The first thing that we do when we are uncomfortable is to judge ourselves and/or others. In that moment you have a choice: you can invest in the judgment or you can suspend your judgment and learn. That is the second

practice: practice suspending your judgments so you can learn. When you do this, you become more capable of seeing your choices. At that point of choice, it is less important what you do as long as you recognize that you are choosing an action; nothing is happening to you, you are choosing.

It marries with our last lesson about the story you tell. Do you see?

Me: Yes. If I know that I am choosing then I cannot tell myself the story that things are happening to me. And, when I know that things aren't happening to me, I'm capable of learning.

Virgil: Exactly. Learning and seeing are conjoined twins. When you can learn, you can see; when you can see, you can learn. For the next week, in addition to working with your two new practices, I have an assignment for you.

Me: Uh-oh. Last time you gave me an assignment I thought you were trying to trick me. ;-)

Virgil: I had to earn your trust before I could start the tricks. Now that you trust me you have to watch out . . . Just kidding. There are no tricks or traps from me. Stepping beyond the known world is full of challenges and traps - but they all come from within you. Rooting out your traps is a necessary part of discovering your patterns of thinking. Here's your assignment: Now that you know that you are telling yourself a story, I want you to pay attention to the many ways in which you 'locate' yourself within the story that you tell. We are constantly locating ourselves in our stories: both physically and in the roles we play. Study how you locate yourself in your story and what that reveals to you.

22.

That was a lot. My head was full. And I was late for a dinner appointment with my friend Bruce so I ran out. I don't like to be late.

When I got to the restaurant Bruce was waiting for me. The waiter asked if we wanted a booth or a table and I saw a table in the corner. I always like to have my back to the wall so I can see what's happening. The moment I asked the waiter for the corner table I realized I was locating myself: I like corner tables. I like my back to the wall. I like to see.

I've known Bruce a long time. We were friends in college. We don't see each other often but I recognized that I was already shifting roles. While I was chatting with Virgil I was a receiver of guidance. Now I was in a new role, listener - a giver of guidance. I was amused to be so aware of my role change. It felt like taking off one mask and replacing it with another. It was seamless! Bruce usually calls when he needs advice or wants to vent about work and I am accustomed to this role; it is comfortable, defined. It is the role I play with him.

I watched Bruce's role change momentarily. He was telling me of his latest frustration at school when the waiter came to the table. Bruce is very knowledgeable about wines and takes great pride in ordering the right wine for us. He instantly transformed into an authority, someone in charge. Once he'd selected the wine, the mask of authority fell away and he once again assumed his role of beleaguered teacher.

Over Bruce's shoulder I saw the waiter, consummate professional with guests, drop his manner when he was behind the bar with the bartender. They were clearly friends and were having a good laugh about something. Then, with the bottle of wine, his professional waiter role resumed, and he approached our table with his waiter mask firmly in place.

This assignment was going to be fun. I already felt as if I was seeing myself in a new light and was now aware of all the other actors that perform in my play.

23.

Parcival, sitting on his mule, having just demanded to be made a knight of the round table, met Arthur's glare with a glare of his own; he didn't know any better. Luckily for him a lady broke the deadly silence. She probably saved his life by declaring, "My lord, I believe this young man will become your greatest knight." Galahad added, "Perhaps. If he lives long enough."

Arthur took a breath. He stared hard at the young man. He recognized him. He was, despite his clownish get-up and his boorish behavior, from noble blood. Arthur could see it. In a very quiet voice, Arthur told Parcival that a man must prove himself worthy by adventures, service and by doing good acts. He told Parcival that he must first learn the code of conduct of a knight. When he had done these things, when he was trained and knighted by a worthy teacher, he would be welcomed back to the court and become a knight of the Round Table.

Parcival wanted nothing more than to be a knight. I wanted nothing more than to be an entrepreneur, a successful businessman. Knight. Entrepreneur. Both are roles. In Virgil speak, both are ways of locating within a story. Parcival wanted to be a knight because, to him, they were godlike; angels shining in their armor, sitting high on their warhorses. I wanted to be an entrepreneur because, to me, they are creators. From nothing they bring forth something that serves people. I'd not recognized that as godlike until this story took me. Now, I recognize that I thought entrepreneurs sat above others, shiny in their minds, all seeing.

Somewhere along the path I stopped seeing. I left school with some book knowledge and a bit of life experience. I stormed into the world thinking I could do anything. No door was closed to me because I had no knowledge of closed doors. There is a freedom that comes from not knowing. When I started to believe that I knew things, when I started believing I was an expert, that I had a sack full of answers for all comers, I slowly stopped seeing. It was what I was taught: be an expert. Stand above others and "know."

I loved this part of the Parcival story because I lived it.

Parcival understood what he had to do. He wheeled his mule around and rode out into the world to prove himself. There are many descriptions of his adventures and they are delicious. He proved to be a redoubtable fighter. No one could best him, and not because he was so highly skilled - because he certainly wasn't - but because he was so loutish, so out of control in combat that he frightened every dark knight, and every dragon or beast that he confronted.

He was a wild boy who knew no fear because he'd never been taught much of anything. Think about it, he had no real armor - most opponents saw this goofy boy wearing dirty broad stripe pajamas and a welcome mat for a breast-plate. His trousers fell more than once. His opponents had a hard time taking him seriously - which was a mistake.

He also had this habit, when juiced with adrenaline - of talking non-stop. He was a talker when calm but amped up considerably when under stress. For instance, whenever he would find a lady held hostage in a tower by an evil knight, he'd start talking. He'd go on and on and on - talking about recipes, hat making, brands of shampoo, it didn't matter - about how best to scale a dragon or fish or a mountain. It's very hard to fight when your opponent won't shut up. Most foes either felt sorry for him - which was a mistake - or they got so irritated at his chatter that they lost their concentration - which was also a mistake.

His natural gifts took him far, just as my gifts took me a long way into business. I'm a natural networker. When I first started I didn't know whom I should fear and whom I should respect. And, because I typically did not do great research, I bumbled into some nice clients who mistook my naivete for honesty and respected me for it.

One famous day an old retired knight named Gornimant was out for a ride when he happened upon Parcival who was engaged in combat with a giant. Now, giants are tough. And apparently, Parcival and the giant had been circling each other for quite some time because, Gornimant later told folks, the giant had this desperate look on his face, the look of someone who is trying to sleep while a mosquito is buzzing around his ears. The giant would swat and Parcival would comment on the giant's combat technique or his choice of club or the giant's posture. Or he would speculate about what it must feel like to have that much hair on his toes. Ultimately, at least this is what Gornimant said, Parcival never struck a blow. He didn't have to because the giant, in desperation, sobbed and surrendered. Parcival actually had to stop the giant from clubbing himself.

Gornimant could recognize potential when he saw it. He'd actually heard of this chattering champion because Parcival was becoming quite famous in the outlands with his trademark chatter. So Gornimant invited Parcival home and promised to teach him the ways of a knight.

The master was good and the student was hungry. Over many months Gornimant taught Parcival the proper use of sword and lance and shield. He taught him the care and feeding of a warhorse, the proper treatment of damsels, which fork to use at the table. But most importantly, he taught him the code and conduct of a knight. Specifically, he taught Parcival to control his chatter, which, up to that point, had been his greatest asset.

Finally, after many long months of study, he presented Parcival with a proper suit of armor, with weapons and a magnificent warhorse. And then Gornimant knighted Parcival in the name of the king.

As Parcival, now a man, prepared to ride away from his master into the world, Gornimant offered his final words of advice. He said, "Talking too much, saying whatever comes into your head, is rude. It is behavior unbecoming of a true knight. Remember, it is impolite for a knight to ask questions. It is rude - even sinful - to speak, without consideration of what comes to your mind."

Having received that final bit of advice, Parcival, thanked

his master and set out for Camelot. But, on the way, he
wanted to go home to show his mother what he'd become.
And, it was only a few weeks later that Parcival came upon
the river and was invited into the Grail Castle by the Fisher
King. Now you know why Parcival failed to ask the Fisher
King about the grail and the lance. For the first time in
his life, Parcival failed, because he did exactly what he had
been taught to do.

Through the story and Virgil's guidance I began to understand that I'd failed for the same reason. My businesses
collapsed because I did exactly what I was taught to do.
And, because I followed the code I'd been given, I stopped
seeing people and what would better their lives. As the
expert, I lived to service my needs and completely forgot
about the needs of my customer.

24.

> **Me**: All week I've been paying attention to
> the roles I play and what happens when I
> assume each role. I have these polar opposite
> sensations like I expand when I assume a role
> and then shrink when I assume another role.
> In some roles I feel like I know things and
> in other roles I feel as if I know nothing. For
> instance, this week I facilitated a workshop
> for young entrepreneurs and, in my role of

facilitator, I was competent, clear, and certain of what I was bringing to the group. As I was leaving the workshop my parents called to check-in and I was suddenly 10 years old again, telling them of the fun day I just had. My language changed, my posture changed, I engaged in an entirely different way in my role as "son."

All week I've asked myself, "why?" Why the dramatic shift in experience from role to role? I'm a bit shocked to realize that I play many, many roles each day. In each role I want something and what I want is different depending upon whom I am with. I realized that my roles are not about me in isolation - and what do I mean by that? I mean that I define my role by how I define the relationship I am in at the moment. For instance, in my workshop, I assumed the role of "guide" and I wanted to lead the young people to some new insights that might help them create their businesses. In my conversation with my parents, in the role of "son," I wanted them to be pleased with my work. I wanted to share and I wanted their approval. So, my role is defined by relationship and in each different relationship I tell a specific story based on what I want or need. I've "cast" myself in these little mini-stories.

Or to use your term, "role" is the way I "locate" myself in the story.

Virgil: And how does this knowledge help you with your questions about business?

Me: The first thing that occurs to me is that I have the capacity to locate myself in a different way if I don't like the role I'm playing. I can change how I locate myself. Also, there is a dance with the words "limitation" and "investment." I took notes all week and realized that I was using the verb "to invest" over and over again to describe my experience of different roles. So, for instance, during my dinner with my friend Bruce I invested in helping him. I wanted Bruce to know that I cared about his challenges. Then, I watched Bruce invest in being the wine expert. It was his way of caring for me and demonstrating his expertise. I began to see my investments as keys to discerning my limitations. In some roles I've invested in the idea that I can't do something or that I'm not good at something. In some roles I diminish myself; my limitations are investments in being small.

Virgil: Just a caution: as you explore further the dance between investment and limitation,

remember to practice suspending your judgment. Remember: you are having experiences
first so you can see how you make meaning
and begin to choose how you make meaning.

Me: Thank you. It's a good reminder. I was
beating myself up every time I realized I was
investing in being small.

Virgil: We tell ourselves stories. We locate
ourselves within the stories. In fact, that is the
next recognition: you locate yourself within
your story. We do it physically (like your
description of choosing the table in the restaurant); we do it through the roles we assume -
specifically our assumptions of how we need
to play our roles, what is ours to do, etc. Locating is simply a way of establishing comfort.
We sort to the known. If you judge how you
locate yourself, you miss the opportunity to
change how you locate yourself.

Me: Right. Judgment blinds me to the choices
I am making.

Virgil: Judgment is always a version of the
"things are happening to me" story. In fact,
judgment is a way of locating: it is the warning

signal when we step too close to discomfort. When I judge myself and say, "I'm an idiot," I'm actually locating myself, pulling myself back into my comfort zone. When I judge others, "They are idiots," I'm locating myself in a higher status position. The action of diminishing "them" elevates me back into a comfortable status position. So, suspending your judgments removes the easy step back to comfort and allows you to stand in "not knowing" and see what is there beyond what you think is there.

The Fourth Recognition: You locate yourself within your story

Study: How do you locate yourself in space? Where do you choose to sit in a movie theatre, on a plane, in a restaurant, in a class? What roles do you play? In each role, what are your investments?

Action: Practice having experiences first and making meaning second.

Exercise: Identify where in your life you carry judgments against yourself and/or other people. Identify the edge signaled by your judgment: name your discomfort. What insights are revealed when you suspend your judgments? What do you see? What choices become available?

Recognition 5: You are the teller of your story

25.

I was now on a journey within my own story.

During our last chat Virgil told me that change is often counterintuitive. For instance, sometimes you must slow down to be more efficient. For me, he said that I needed to work on my "being" if I ever wanted to succeed in my "doing."

I am now seeing the roles I choose. I am discovering the agenda beneath each role. I see what I need and what I want. I see when I manipulate. I see where I place limits on myself. I see where I remove them. I'm learning to recognize my investments.

Early in our work together it was my habit to get angry after my chats with Virgil. I wanted answers! I wanted to understand. The last thing I wanted was to "not know" what I was doing. My anger revealed my judgments. "Not knowing" made me uncomfortable. "Not knowing" felt vulnerable, exposed. I got angry because I told myself the story that Virgil was responsible for my discomfort. He was the cause, not me. It was easier to blame him than it was to own my feelings.

When I learned to suspend my judgments I saw why I was so angry. For me, to know is like armor; "knowing" is my protection. I've never really innovated because I've never willingly stepped into the unknown. I was guarded against ever stepping into discomfort so I was guarded against learning, growing, seeing, innovating, and creating. Virgil exposed the truth: I do not know.

In my life to this point I was always perceived as the one who knew what to do. I was always rewarded for knowing what to do. I was taught in school that a good businessperson has a plan and he follows the plan; he knows where he is going and he knows what he is doing. I believed I was a good businessperson. As Virgil wrote, "That's old-world thinking." The whole equation has flipped because the river is moving too fast. Have the experience first. Act. And then make meaning. Act. Test. And then Aim. See the patterns.

People who think they know look for problems. People who understand that they do not know see patterns and create.

My business failed. I did not. I learned. I am learning.

When I emailed this to Virgil he told me that the fifth recognition was very close at hand. He said it was a nuance, a subtle addition to the recognitions that have come before. He congratulated me for beginning the process of removing my armor. He wrote:

> **Virgil**: Everyday you get closer and closer to actually seeing.

26.

Parcival failed in the Fisher King's castle because he did as he was taught to do. He heeded Gornimant's advice. He lived within the code as the only way to fulfill his heart's desire. Like me, he stopped seeing. Like me, he cut himself off from his nature.

The Fisher King gave Parcival a sword. The detail of the story that I play over and over in my mind is the maiden coming out of the woods and telling him his name: Parcival the Unfortunate. She also warned him that the sword, the gift from the king, would fail him when he most needed it.

I wondered what was my sword? What was my destiny? How had my sword failed me when I needed it most?

Parcival was confused and ashamed. Remember, he immediately sought Arthur's court for help and guidance. He entered the court wearing his shiny new armor and carrying a new sword. And before he could ask anyone to explain what had happened in the castle, the loathly damsel entered, denounced him, stripped him naked before the whole court, and blamed him for the horrors to come.

Parcival was more confused and more ashamed than ever. He left Arthur's court, with all eyes avoiding him. He left vowing never to rest in the same place for two nights until he found the Grail Castle again and set things aright.

He kept his vow, too. For five years he searched for the Grail Castle. He was, as they say, completely in the field of action. He was a knight. A warrior. He rescued damsels. He defeated dark knights. He conquered ogres and giants and dragons. He liberated villages from curses and cretins. And during those five years, despite his best efforts, the crone's prophecy still came true. Many knights died. The land became barren. People starved. Children were orphaned. Widows mourned their losses. It seemed that the more Parcival searched, the harder he looked, the more he tried to prove his worth, the more independent he became, the more devastated and empty was his world. Which made him fight harder to prove himself worthy. He thought that if he sacrificed himself he could keep the land alive.

Have you ever been so good at something and wanted to

succeed so badly that you unknowingly compromise your self? Your work becomes about proving yourself instead of serving others? You find, one day, that everything you've strived to create is empty and you are living out of balance. That's what happened to me. I was working so hard to prove myself that I forgot why I was doing what I was doing.

Parcival also forgot the object of his quest. He forgot that he was searching to find the Grail Castle. He became filled with a kind of fervor, zeal. Every act became an act of redemption. Every action was an exploit to prove his worth.

No one and nothing could defeat him in battle. He became famous! People talked of his sword, this magic sword, and after awhile even he came to believe the sword was the source of his power.

The parallels between the story and my life are startling! That is why stories are so useful: learn to see the patterns and read the metaphors and you will see yourself in them. The metaphors open when the story takes you. This is what I see: in my business, every action was intended to prove my worth. And, like Parcival, I invested my power, my safety and security in an illusion. Parcival came to believe his sword was the source of his power and I came to believe that my intellect, my knowing, was the source of my power. My knowledge was my sword and I wielded it like a weapon. Tim had tried gently to explain why our primary client dropped us: I was the reason. I was too much the expert. I became a fixer, an answer man who had no time to hear the client's story.

Stories often turn on the moment when the main character learns how drastically he has separated himself from himself. Trying to prove worth is an act of separation. Investing in an illusion like a magic sword or sharp knowledge is an act of separation. It reinforces the belief that our power is external to us. Worth is not something that can be proved or attained. It is in us all along.

This is what happens to illusions:

On a famous day, while riding through the forest, out of the trees rode a warrior like none that Parcival had ever seen. The warrior didn't wear armor, his skin was dark, and he somehow belonged to the land. He was an enormous man. He moved like a panther, beautiful, easy, fluid, and confident. He sat atop a black stallion. He squared himself to Parcival and drew his sword for battle.

Parcival surprised himself; he did not want to fight this man. He felt a deep sadness and was suddenly very tired. He told the warrior that he would not fight. He asked the warrior to stand aside and let him pass. The warrior stood his ground. Parcival said that he had no quarrel and would not draw his weapon. The man said nothing and stood his ground. Slowly Parcival drew his sword, thinking that once his sword was seen, the warrior would recognize Parcival and retreat. The man saw the sword and stood his ground.

Parcival felt as though he could not breath. They stared for a long moment, sizing up each other, and then, silently, as if in agreement, they suddenly rode at each other. Their swords met with a ferocious clang that echoed off the trees and hills. The impact knocked both men off their mounts. Parcival landed hard. Like a turtle on his back, pinned down by the weight of his armor, Parcival looked up and saw the warrior, the panther, standing over him, raising his sword to strike. Parcival raised his sword in defense and found he held only the hilt of his weapon. His sword, the Fisher King's gift, had exploded into a thousand pieces.

27.

I went to my local bookstore to pick up something I ordered. Andrew, the owner, gave me my book. There was a slip of paper folded and tucked inside the pages. My name was printed in marker on the outside fold. I said, "What's this?" Andrew looked at it and said, "It's for you, I guess. I don't know how it got there."

I opened it and found a postcard bearing the black and white image of a factory with this quote:

"The story of the human race is the story of men and women selling themselves short." Abraham Maslow

28.

On my way walking home from the bookstore I was almost hit by a car. Well, I was hit, but the driver was paying attention and I ended up sitting on the hood instead of flying through the air as I might have done had the driver not seen me. It was my fault. I was thinking about the quote and I was wondering how someone knew that I had a book to pick up. How did they get the quote into my book? I was reading and rereading the quote when I stepped into traffic. I heard the brakes and instinctively jumped. It was as if the car scooted under me like a chair and I was suddenly sitting on the hood. I started laughing.

The driver jumped out of the car and was at first scared and then surprised and angry at my laughter, and then, when he realized that I was okay, he sat on the hood with me. A small crowd formed to see what was going to happen. The driver said, "You scared me to death."

I said, "Thanks for paying attention. I was so lost in thought that I forgot where I was."

He laughed and stood up. "This will make a great story for my wife. 'Hi honey, I hit someone today and we had a nice chat on the hood of the car.'" He offered me his hand.

I said, "You could tell this story in a thousand different ways and keep her on the hook for an hour."

"I think I'll exaggerate it a bit. I'll tell her you're some kind of acrobat and flipped through the air onto the hood. You sure you're okay?" he asked.

"I'm fine. And I'm grateful that you saw me. Thanks for the seat!" I jumped off the hood and stepped back onto the curb.

"Anytime!" he said, getting back into the car. The crowd dispersed as he drove away.

I stood on the corner suddenly aware of the fifth recognition. It was subtle, just as Virgil promised. I am the teller of my story. I give it shape. I give it meaning. I give it coherence. I exaggerate it. I hang onto parts of it. I define the limits. My story is not happening to me. I am creating it as I go, based on my investments and assumptions of my roles and how I choose to play them. I'm focusing on certain aspects of my story and ignoring others.

In every moment I'm doing what the driver will do when he goes home to his wife. He will tell a story of an experience.

Later that evening Virgil wrote:

> **Virgil**: Within circumstance you are always in choice. And the first choice you have is the story you decide to tell. You are the teller of your story. This may sound simplistic but the recognition that you are in every moment, every day, responsible for the story you tell, is enormously powerful.

> **Me**: I felt it as I stood on the street corner. In fact, I stood there for a long time watching people, watching them play their roles within the stories they tell. I watched mothers with children, people hurrying home from work, couples taking a stroll, kids hurrying to soccer

practice. All were deeply invested in their story. It was subtle as you said, but the small progression from knowing that I am telling a story to actually owning that I am the teller of my story was . . . huge.

Virgil: Why was it huge?

Me: What I saw in others, and then saw for myself, was a real commitment to the story. There was a dedication to the circumstance. Here's that word again: an investment that the story was fact or reality. They were seeing their story and nothing beyond it.

Virgil: Yes, the commitment to our stories blinds us to potential. Have you ever come across the phrase "premature cognitive commitment"?

Me: No.

Virgil: It is how elephants are trained to stay in one place. The process is almost too simple: when it is young, a baby, a strong chain is wrapped around its ankle. The other end of the chain is secured to a very strong tree. The baby elephant will pull and pull against the chain but soon learns that there is no use pulling, so it stops testing the chain. As it grows, weaker and weaker chains are used and attached to smaller and smaller trees. Since the elephant has learned that it is no use to pull on the chain, eventually a piece of string attached to a tiny stick is all that is required to keep the elephant from roaming free. The idea of limitation, the story that it is no use pulling on the string, is more powerful than the reality of the string and the stick. Many of the stories we tell are premature cognitive commitments; we become so dedicated to our limits that we stop testing what we think we know.

Me: When I recognize that I am the teller of my own story, I have the capacity to challenge my assumptions. I never stop pulling on the chain to see what will happen.

Virgil: Yes, and, in that way, you see what is there, not what you think is there. You have the opportunity to see beyond your story or at least you are capable of choosing the story you tell. Why should the limit that you experienced as a child dictate your range of motion as an adult? What commitments do we make that keep us from testing the chain? These are the same commitments that prohibit us from seeing.

The Fifth Recognition: You are the teller of your story

Study: Actions reveal choices, choices reveal story. Study your actions and your choices: what story do they reveal?

Action: Own your story. Continue to distinguish the difference between circumstance and story. Eliminate the "things happen to me" story: at the end of each day choose an event from the day that was challenging, frustrating or made you mad. What if your response within every circumstance was a choice? What did you choose within your circumstance? Track it each day in your journal. What changes when your choices become conscious and intentional?

Exercise: Identify your commitment to limits. Be specific. Identify one limit in which you've invested. Pull on the chain. What are your rules? Challenge them. Cross a boundary. What happens? Track it in your journal.

Recognition 6: You can change your story

29.

When my business failed my confidence collapsed. Like Parcival's sword, everything that I thought I knew was worthless and lay in pieces all around me.

I stayed in bed wallowing in my misery for a week with my blankets pulled over my head. When finally I realized that I had nothing else to lose, I got out of bed and called Elizabeth. My business was gone, my pride, my reputation, my intention, my identity. I was pinned down and had no fight left in me. I surrendered. And that was when I found Virgil.

It seemed that the Parcival story was a braid strand entwined with my life story. Was I following the story or was the story following me?

Parcival's sword exploded. The pieces of his power lay all around him.

The panther, the warrior of the earth, stood above Parcival poised and ready to strike the fatal blow. Parcival was pinned down by the weight of his armor. Laying on his back, he looked up into the warrior's eyes, surrendering himself to death. He closed his eyes thinking, this is going to hurt. Nothing happened. Parcival opened his eyes and the warrior, like the castle and the maiden, was gone. Parcival managed to roll onto his knees and something broke inside him. He wept.

After the warrior vanished, Parcival retreated deeper into the woods. In his five years of searching he'd become intensely self-reliant. He couldn't go back to court. He had no idea how to get home. The source of all his power had just been shattered. His life was not unfolding as he had imagined that day long ago, when he first bumped into the knights and confused them with gods and he decided that he, too, would become a knight.

While he was deep in his despair, he was discovered by a hermit. Now, it's harder to be discovered by a hermit than you might imagine. A hermit, by definition, likes to be alone and generally avoids contact with other people. The hermit found Parcival just as Gornimant had found him. Parcival was ready for his next life lessons so his teacher emerged.

That's the same story I tell myself about Virgil. I was ready and he emerged. Elizabeth had given me Virgil's contact information a few months before I emailed him. I wasn't ready to learn until I experienced the collapse of my business. Just like Parcival, I needed to lose my sword before I was ready for the teacher to find me.

Parcival was sitting on a stump, helmet off, weeping - which was why he retreated deeper into the woods because he didn't want to be seen. It was the perfect time for a hermit to come along. I think the sight of a knight in full armor, sitting on a stump having a barking-style cry got the best of the hermit. It piqued his curiosity.

Hermits are notoriously quiet so Parcival didn't hear the hermit sit down on the stump next to him. You can imagine his surprise, after his cry had run its course, when he heard a crackly old voice say, "That's a hell of a giant you're fighting in there. What's his name?" Parcival yelped and jumped from his stump. Keep in mind that this story is happening in the days when forest spirits showed themselves to mortals. Parcival wasn't sure if he was about to be spelled or cursed. When he jumped up, he landed sideways on his foot and, being in full armor, he made the sound that a stack of cans in a grocery store makes when a cart bumps into it. He kind of looked like that too, as he crumpled all the way to the ground.

The hermit chuckled and said, "Simmer down boy. I'm not going to turn you into a frog or nothing. I'm a hermit!"

That was not very comforting although it did help Parcival relax a bit. The hermit helped Parcival out of his armor so he could stand. The hermit looked him over, and invited Parcival back to the cave for some stew. Parcival went with the hermit, leaving his armor behind.

He broke his vow not to stay two nights in the same place until he found the Grail Castle again. Parcival stayed with the hermit for a night, then two, then he lost count of how long he'd been there. You've probably guessed by now that the hermit was his second master. The first master teaches craft. Second masters are the midwives for the birth of the heart.

30.

Virgil wrote:

> **Virgil**: The sixth recognition is a gateway. Just as the third recognition completed a cycle called "pattern," the sixth completes a second loop called "story." Do you see we are making a Venn diagram with three circles?

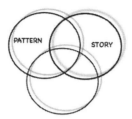

Me: Yes. What is the third cycle called?

Virgil: Not so fast. We will get there soon enough. First you must complete the story cycle. Given what you know about the recognitions that comprise this cycle: #4: you locate yourself within your story and #5: you are the teller of your story, can you guess what comes next, what is the logical next step?

Me: What I realized almost immediately was that, as the teller of my story, I have the capacity to change my story. I can choose the story I want to tell.

Virgil: Yes, that's it. The sixth recognition is "you can change your story." It is an easy concept to grasp but, like all simplicities, it can be hard to do. The work that you have done so far learning about patterns, investments, attachments, roles, and locating, is a first step. It is something you must continue if you desire to master the capacity to change your story. I've also given you three practices:

1) Practice "Not Knowing" (practice curiosity).

2) Practice having an experience first, then make meaning of the experience second.

3) Practice suspending your judgment so you can learn.

Before we leave this cycle there is a fourth practice to add:

4) Practice controlling what you can control and letting the rest go.

Me: I'm not sure I understand.

Virgil: Investments, attachments, and many limiting patterns are the result of trying to control things in your life over which you have no control. People spend great amounts of their lives trying to control what they cannot control. So, first you must identify what you can and cannot control. After you've identified what you can control, begin the practice of focusing your actions and choices toward what you can change. And, stop trying to change what you cannot.

Me: This seems . . . overwhelming.

Virgil: Start simply. Begin with a sheet of paper. Draw a line down the center of the paper. On one side at the top write: Things I can control. On the other side, write: Things I need to let go. Add to your list every day and soon you will clearly see what is within your control and what is not.

31.

I went to the coffee house to do the exercise Virgil suggested. It quickly became very clear that there are not many things that I can control. For instance, I can't control what other people think or feel or believe. This was the big revelation. At the table next to me I heard a woman say, "I don't want him to think I'm a bad person."

How much time have I invested in my life in the idea that I can determine what another person thinks? Too much! How often have I said, "I don't want them to think that I . . .," or "I don't want them to feel . . . ."

I was beginning to see the true value of this exercise: my emotional, mental and physical health is invested in something over which I have no control. No wonder I'm stressed all the time. No wonder we fall into the "things happen to me" story! My energy is wasted if I am trying to control another person's thoughts or feelings.

During my dinner with Bruce, he was deeply upset because he believed his principal didn't like him. He said, "I know she doesn't like me." I asked how he knew and he said, "She's cold to me. I think she just wants me to fall in line and stop agitating for the elimination of the tests." When I asked if he'd talked to her, if he'd asked her about what she believed, he said, "No! I can't do that! She'd think I was manipulating or something. I want her to see that I'm a good teacher and that I care first and foremost about the kids."

There is so much miscommunication and confusion all in the name of trying to control what another person sees or thinks.

More things I can't control: I can't control market forces or the weather. I can't control traffic. Why do I get so angry when I am stuck in traffic? Is there anything I can do about it? No! I can't control prices, my brother's mania, the education system . . . This list is endless.

The list of things I can control, by comparison, is very short. I can control what I think. I can control the actions I take. I can control the story I tell. That's it. Everything else on the list is a subset of my thoughts, my actions, or my story.

Virgil's message was clear: If I want to change my story I first must stop trying to control what I can't control. And, if the only things over which I have control are my thoughts and my actions, then that is where the change to my story must begin.

If the point of this entire process is to make me a better businessperson, to help me become successful, then I have to stop investing in the premise that my ideas have worth or not, that I am either a success or failure, that "not knowing" what to do is a reason to stand still. On the contrary, it is the very reason to step out and try anything. How did Virgil say it? Act. Test. Then aim.

32.

You can change your story. That is the sixth recognition. Doesn't it sound simple? Say it this way: changing your story is the equivalent of changing who you know yourself to be. Changing your story often requires the loss of your illusion, a lot less armor and nothing left to lose. Who are you when you don't know who you are or where you are going? This was the heart of Virgil's question to me. Who are you distinct from your circumstance? Who are you when the mask comes off? More importantly, what are you capable of seeing when you are not looking through a visor?

No one is immune to the stuff of life. Everyone lives a unique version of the story cycle. It too is a pattern, a natural process.

I was surprised when looking through my mail I found a postcard. The image was a watercolor painting of a snake.

On the back, in blue ink, I found this quote from Friedrich Nietzsche:

"The snake which cannot cast its skin has to die. As well the minds which are prevented from changing their opinions; they cease to be a mind."

33.

This is the part of the Parcival story where I realized what Virgil's role was in my life. It was uncanny. I was suffering the exact fears and frustrations as Parcival. And, I was coming to the same lesson. I was starting to see. The story continues to unfold.

It took an amazing amount of courage for Parcival to sit still and even more courage to listen to that deep inner voice that said, "Don't run. This hermit has something for you, but if you stay, you'll never be the same again." It was a kind of death. It was frustrating. It was crazy-making. It was scary and the hermit tended to laugh a lot in response to Parcival's fears and frustrations. This didn't help matters much at all.

Parcival kept waiting for the hermit to give him "the lesson" or "the answer" just as I waited for Virgil to tell me what to do. Parcival believed that the hermit had an answer or at the very least some advice but was waiting to deliver it because Parcival was not yet ready. So Parcival waited. And somewhere in the process, Parcival began to slow down. He stopped defining himself by his doing. He no longer knew himself as a knight. He completely forgot about dragons and ogres. He no longer needed to rescue anyone. He no longer needed to prove his worth or disappear into service. He even forgot about waiting for the hermit's advice. He became much more than a role or an action. He let go of any notion of *fulfilling* a purpose and slowly *became* his purpose. He put down his "knowing" and was soon filled with bewilderment and curiosity.

He flipped. He practiced "not knowing."

He changed his story because he changed himself.

No one really knows how long he stayed with the hermit, months or maybe years. No one knows what he did with all that time. His power was no longer in a sword. What we do know is that one day, while helping the hermit carry wood to the cave, he heard a noise and turned to find the Grail Castle standing in the meadow just behind him. The drawbridge was coming down. He could see the faces of the lords and ladies. They were excited to see him, almost as if they were expecting him.

Startled, Parcival looked to the hermit. He didn't know if he was imagining things or if the hermit saw it, too. The hermit smiled and said, "Boy, it has been there all along."

The Sixth Recognition: You can change your story

Study: Identify the things you can and can't control.

Draw a line down the center of a piece of paper. Label one side "Things I Can Control." Label the other side, "Things I Can't Control and Need to Let Go." Add to the list everyday as you discover what you can and can't control.

Action: Focus your efforts on what you can control. Use the list of "Things You Can Control" to clarify your actions and intentions. Continue to add to the list.

Exercise: Choose one thing from the "Can't Control" list and let it go. Begin practicing letting go of the things you cannot control. Continue to identify what is out of your control and let it go.

Cycle Three: Choice

Recognition 7: You are always in Choice

34.

Virgil: Trace the path that we've followed and name for me the six recognitions.

Me: The first three recognitions constitute the loop called Pattern. They are:

- I don't have a problem. I have a pattern.

- My language matters. It is a pattern that defines my story.

- I am telling myself a story. My story is a pattern that determines what I see.

You asked me to surface my patterns because pattern reveals story.

The next three recognitions constitute the loop called Story. They are:

- I locate myself within a story. The emphasis is "I locate."

- I am the teller of my story. The most important location to recognize is as the storyteller of my story.

- Because I am the storyteller, I can change my story.

Virgil: Good. You are ready to move forward now. The third loop is called Choice and it is mostly invisible until you understand and embrace the first six recognitions. To change your story, you must first recognize that you are in choice every single moment of every day.

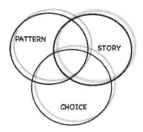

Me: Is this the 7th recognition?

Virgil: Yes. Everything we've done so far was meant to help you see how you are always choosing. Your story is a choice. Do you recall a distinction I made recently about control: you may not be able to control your circumstance but you have infinite control over how you are within your circumstance?

Me: Yes.

Virgil: The "infinite control" you have within your circumstance is called Choice. Do you also remember in an earlier conversation that I wrote about how a complexity can never be changed with another complexity but that significant change is always realized through a series of small simplicities?

Me: Yes, I remember. You wrote that it's the little steps, the things that look insignificant that cumulatively create great change.

Virgil: Exactly. The little steps are the small choices that you make - all those things that you think are insignificant - they are very powerful choices.

Me: Can you give me an example?

Virgil: I will give you an exercise and this week you can find examples to share with me.

Me: Fair enough!

Virgil: After you learn to draw a line between what you can control and what you cannot control, there is a necessary second distinction to be made. Earlier you developed the capacity to hear two different kinds of stories. Now you need to hear them within yourself and distinguish between the two. The exercise is simple: draw a line down the center of a piece of paper. At the top of the left side write: "Things happen to me." On the other side write: "I make things happen." Simply pay attention to and capture the moments in your life when 1) you think things are happening to you and, 2) you make things happen. People move toward choice and away from blaming when they can distinguish between these two points of view.

Me: Can you say more about choice and blame? How are choice and blame related? This may seem obvious, but it already rings a bell concerning my business collapse. Everyone - including me - blamed someone for what happened.

Virgil: In the previous exercise, drawing a line between what we can and can't control helps us orient toward actions that matter. It clarifies our relationships, creating relationships of mutual empowerment and cleans up enabling relationships (eliminates them). Letting go of what we can never control creates space and frees the energy that is necessary for moving along the spectrum toward clarity and empowerment. As we walk toward power we begin to see our relationship with choice. It is common for people to "let go of what they can't control" but to stop short of owning what they can control. They stop short of choice. Letting go is the easy part. Owning our choices is where the work really begins. It is where the real creative power lives. It is what distinguishes an effectual entrepreneur from the rest of the crowd. In this exercise, drawing a line between the experiences in which you think things are happening to you (blame stories) and experiences in which you believe you are making things happen (stories of choice) reveals your patterns of blame: where you do not yet own your choices. It clarifies where you are standing relative to your creative power. Ultimately, it will free you from patterns of blame. It supports you in seeing that you are always choosing, every minute, every day.

35.

At first I thought this was going to be easy. See my choices. Own my choices. Why not, right? Given the capacity to see choice, who doesn't want to create his empowerment? Just assume it! Claim it! Just do it. Isn't that what Virgil said? I set up my piece of paper, drew the line down the middle and wrote on the left: "Things happen to me!" On the right side at the top, I wrote: "I make things happen!" Both titles seemed like declarations when I wrote them. I imagined two cartoons for the headers: on the left, a cartoon salesman briefcase akimbo, papers blowing everywhere, hands clenched, and shouting, "AAARGH! Why do things always happen to me?" The image made me laugh.

The other side, the "I make things happen" side brought the cartoon image of a caveman carving the world's first wheel; his buddies standing behind him, commenting, "What do you think will happen?"

I identified with the wheel maker. I was certain my choice story list would grow while my blame story list would languish.

And then life happened. Later that afternoon, I was late leaving for an appointment and I couldn't find my keys. I usually run late so leaving the house is always a hurricane of activity and suddenly I couldn't find my keys. I tore open drawers, rummaged through coat pockets, checked and rechecked counter tops and my desk. I was furious and stopped cold when I shouted, "Why does this always happen to me!" I was the cartoon salesman. I stomped to my piece of paper and wrote "lost keys" on the list of "things happen to me."

The next morning my neighbor mowed his lawn at 7:00am. It was Saturday morning and I was trying to sleep in. I got angry. "Great!" I shouted. Burying my head in my pillow I grumbled, "Of course. This always happens when I want to sleep!" I sat up when I heard what I said. My story: this early morning mowing was happening to me. I got out of bed, stomped over to my list and added, "Inconsiderate-neighbor-early-morning-mowing" to the list of "things happen to me."

How can I make things happen if I can't find my keys? How is a story of choice possible when the choice I want to make is to throw stones at the old man living next door?

As the week went on I saw how often I live a blame story. I honk my horn and curse at other drivers for driving too slowly, as if they were doing it to irritate me. When I couldn't find strawberries in the grocery store because they ran out, I felt like they ran out of strawberries just to irritate me. The left side of my list, the blame side, grew. The right side, choice, also grew but it seemed as if the two lists were describing two totally different people, two totally different identities.

I emailed Virgil and told him of the split personality I perceived. This is what he wrote back:

> **Virgil:** Check your assumptions.

That's it. That was all he sent. I got angry. Of course. Anger is my first step when I feel stuck. I wanted an answer and when I feel blocked I get angry. I even went so far as to rant at my screen, "What? Check your own assumptions! Why is an answer to my question too much to give me?" And then I heard it. I heard the blame story in my rant. I believed this was happening to me. I slowly added to the list, "Wanting an answer to my question."

I put my head on the desk. This assignment seemed impossible.

I was beginning to see my pattern and I didn't like what I saw.

After a few hours I calmed down and realized that although I'd passed through the first six recognitions I was still reacting to circumstance and often felt out of control. When I lost my keys I felt anxious. In my mind I played a frantic story about the repercussions of being late for my appointment - and it was a doctor's appointment, not a client or a friend in distress. No one was dying so why did I tell such a dire story? Why did I jump into a story of the universe plotting against me? It was as if I entertained the idea that someone slipped into my house and hid my keys just to make me crazy. It was a plot. It was happening to me. I was a victim. The victim story was full to overflowing with accusations against myself: I was an idiot. Why couldn't I do the simplest thing like keep track of my keys? The more I thought about it the more absurd it seemed. It was as if I was the persecutor and the victim of persecution. Another variation of the split personality!

The pattern began to come clear. When I felt out of control or blocked from a goal I told a story of blame. I cast myself as a victim in the story. It's as if the blame story relieved me of any responsibility for my choices. I was out of control so things were happening to me. Being blocked became my story. I invested in the idea that the forces were allied against me. I told the story that I was surrounded by idiots or, worse, I *was* the idiot. When I jumped into my blame story, inner warfare was the result. I had no choice but to fight, push, resist, defend, attack, or retreat. It felt as if I fractured and fell into warring pieces. More splits. I could see nothing but turmoil and injustice. In this story I had no choice because I couldn't see my choices.

What made it worse was there was never any truth to the story I whipped up. For instance, the day I lost my keys I was late for a doctor's appointment. The doctor regularly keeps me waiting. In fact, I expect to be kept waiting so I always schedule plenty of time around my appointments! So why would I panic about *possibly* being a few minutes late to the doctor? I found my keys. They were in the bottom of my shoulder bag. The actual delay might have been five minutes and despite my story of shame and woe, despite my extreme stress and self-abuse, I arrived on time for my appointment! I waited twenty-five minutes before I was called in to an examination room. Why would I tell a story of "things happen to me," creating so much stress, instead of telling a story of choice? I had plenty of choices. I could have chosen to slow down and breathe. I could have called the doctor's office and let them know I was running late. I could have made the life changing choice of not rushing to get out of the door every time I leave my house. When in a blame story I could not see my choices or I refused to see them. Owning them was impossible.

I realized how easy it is to invest in blame stories. Blame is easy. Choice is more demanding.

Virgil wrote that I should check my assumptions. At first it made me mad. I assumed he was withholding something I needed. I assumed he was in control of what I wanted. I wrote the words "splits" and "separations" on my yellow pad. Then I wrote the word, "power."

I was creating separations. I was creating splits and fragments.

As I looked at my list of "things happen to me," I saw in every circumstance my assumptions that someone had power over me. The neighbor mowing the lawn was responsible for my happiness. The doctor's time was more valuable than mine. The woman that cut me off in traffic was diminishing me; I made her responsible for my feelings. None of the stories were true. None of the stories existed anywhere outside of me. I assumed I was being controlled. I assumed powerlessness so my actions were reactionary.

Virgil said that this loop was about choice and my "relationship with Choice." I was beginning to see that my relationship with choice was also about my relationship with power. Did I recognize my capacity to create my story? Did I truly understand and own my power to define my experiences? Sometimes yes and sometimes no! I had a hot and cold relationship with choice. It was a relationship of convenience. I told a story of choice when it suited me, when I was successful. I told a story of blame when things were tough. When my business was going well, I was a genius. When it collapsed it wasn't my fault. It happened to me.

I read again my last chat with Virgil. He wrote:

> **Virgil:** [the exercise] reveals your patterns of blame: where you do not yet own your choices. It clarifies where you are standing relative to your creative power. Ultimately, it will free you from patterns of blame. It supports you in seeing that you are always choosing, every minute, every day.

When I think about the neighbor's early morning mowing

I recognize that waking up from a deep sleep to a lawn mower just outside my window was circumstance. My anger was a normal reaction. Virgil was asking me to consider the choices I had within the circumstance. What I chose to do was blame. I chose to complain to myself. I chose to invest in a victim story. I chose not to go talk to my neighbor. The single action that might help was the only thing I chose not to do.

I returned to my original list of things that I can and cannot control. I wrote on the "Can't Control and Need to Let Go" column: I can't control the neighbor's mowing habits. I can control how I respond to them. More to Virgil's point: I can control how I choose to respond. If I understood that I was in choice every minute of every day, would my first response always be anger? In fact, now I saw that anger might be a signal that I was telling a story of blame.

This insight was radical to me: I have choice in how I respond. I do not have to lapse into anger. My anger, my response, was rooted in the assumption that I couldn't do anything about my circumstance. My anger was rooted in the assumption that I was being victimized. In situations like the lost keys or the neighbor mowing, I couldn't see my relationship with Choice because I assumed that I had no choices. I was a victim of an insensitive neighbor. I was a victim to my idiot-self losing my keys.

The implications for my business were ominous. I was slow to pivot when my original plan wasn't working. I needed to be right. I had "to know." So I was rigid when I needed to be flexible. I was slow to pivot because I was invested in blame stories! I didn't want to be blamed if things didn't go well. My need to be right was actually an abdication of responsibility. It's hard to modify and change direction when justifying or defending a course of action. I suddenly saw how a consistent relationship with choice would have opened my eyes. Choice is nimble. Blame is rigid.

I once had a client who refused to make business cards. In a fit of honesty he confessed to me, "It gives me a back door! If my business fails I can say to myself, 'I didn't do everything that I could do to succeed. If only I'd made business cards!'" He smiled at his self-directed blame story. Blame stories are games meant to relieve us of responsibility.

I didn't like what I saw in my assumptions. I assumed that I had no choices. I assumed that things were happening to me and I completely missed that I was capable of making things happen, as I wanted them to happen.

Virgil was trying to get me to see that I had choice in how I oriented myself to my life and my business.

> It was so simple: to choose is to create. To blame assumes that I have no choices.

Virgil's exercise was a next step toward seeing. If I focus on what I can control and let the rest go, I don't get enmeshed in control games - with myself or other people. If I orient toward choice and become conscious of the choices available to me each and every moment, I know without a doubt that I am creating. Always. I cease to blame.

What if, instead of flying off into a rage and choosing the victim role, I made coffee, took the neighbor a cup, and I asked him next time to wait until eight o'clock in the morning to mow? I laughed when I ran through the possible choices. I could mow the yard for my neighbor or pay my lawn service to mow his yard and pay them extra to start after 10am. Why not? What if I communicated with him before accusing him? What if I used this circumstance as an opportunity to get to know him better? What if we actually collaborated on being good neighbors? What if we acted as if being neighbors was a relationship that required communication and careful tending? What if we saw a process and not a fixed outcome?

The next simplicity dawned on me: when I focus on choice, I focus on process and relationship. When I convince myself that I have no choices, I focus on outcomes. I fool myself into thinking that there is an arrival platform called "Happiness" and that I may or may not achieve it someday.

Virgil asked me to check my assumptions. Our assumptions reveal how we orient to our lives. It looped back to the exercise. I looked at my list and considered my two cartoon characters: 1) the salesman oriented to the belief that things are happening to him and 2) the caveman oriented to the understanding that he makes things happen.

Both are basic assumptions and patterns of action, patterns of choices follow.

It is a matter of how you orient. It matters how you choose to see. If I assume choice, then I must also assume responsibility. When I orient to choice I will no longer be buffeted by circumstance. Success won't be an accident or something that happens someday. When fully living in choice, success is something I create.

36.

So, I was absolutely thunderstruck when I made coffee and took it to my neighbor. He said, "Oh, this came for you but they delivered it to the wrong house." He handed me a small box. I opened it and found a page torn from a book. This phrase was circled:

"It's not our talents that make us safe or dangerous, it's our choices."

Josephine Angelini, Dreamless

I went home and completely forgot to talk to him about mowing so early in the morning.

37.

The Grail Castle is a metaphor. Attaining the grail is a metaphor. Mastering metaphor is necessary for a story to open and be fully understood. Each of us, every human being, is both Parcival and the Grail Castle. We seek ourselves. And, to find ourselves we have to learn to see again. We have to leave behind our list of "should dos;" we have to stop seeking our answers in other people and instead look to ourselves; we need to drop our armor and let go of our weapons. We need to return to our natural curiosity and capacity to "not know." We need to own our choices.

When Parcival entered the castle the second time, it was exactly as it had been the first time. It was as if no time had passed. He was different. He entered unguarded, without role or expectation. He had nothing to hide and nothing to lose. He entered, not as the boy filled with self importance nor the knight singly dedicated to a code of service to others. He had no armor, no weapons and no other place to be.

Just as before, the lords and ladies greeted him joyfully. They embraced him and then led him to the great hall to meet the Fisher King. The King, just as before, lay on a great couch, wrapped in a sumptuous robe before a warming fire. He was in terrible, unceasing pain.

The lords and ladies, all the members of the court, entered the great hall, every heart filled with expectation. All eyes were on Parcival.

Parcival, without an invitation, sat on the couch next to the king and a hush fell over the assembly. Just then, the young man came into the hall. He carried the lance, the same as before, brilliant white, with a single bead of blood that ran from its tip down the shaft and almost but not quite touched the young man's hand. Parcival watched the young man process across the hall and disappear out the far door. This time, when the assembly turned and stared at Parcival, their eyes filled with expectation, he looked to the King and asked, "Sir, I do not understand what you show me. Can you tell me what this means? Can you tell me what ails you? Why are you in such pain?" The Fisher King smiled. Tears filled the eyes of the gathered host and streamed down their cheeks. The King's face flushed red, the pain left his body and his health was instantly restored.

Then, just as happened before, two more men entered the great hall, each carrying candelabra with hundreds of burning candles. The light from the candles filled every corner of the great hall. And behind them came the girl. She held the golden bowl. As before, it shone so brilliantly that its warm radiance filled the room and its light was so bright that the candles could no longer be seen. All were transfixed. Parcival stood up and looked directly into the eyes of the King and asked, "Sir, why do you show me this? Whom does the grail serve?"

It was in front of me all along. What is the difference in Parcival's first and second experiences in the castle? It is such a small thing! Parcival asks his questions; he does not suppress them or let them burn. He is not victim to his code. The experience is not happening to him; he is making things happen.

38.

Me: It seems like such a small thing and yet it is monumental! I now see clearly how small things create big changes. I was incapable of talking to my neighbor because I *assumed* conflict and manufactured the illusion that I was a victim and as a victim I was incapable of acting. I could react. I could resist. I could blame. I could be angry and as a victim I was justified in my anger; things were happening to me. The one thing I was not able to see was my choices. I couldn't see possibilities, options or how I was orienting myself.

Virgil: Yes - and I want to feed this back to you because what you are discovering is central to everything we've been exploring: when you cannot see your capacity for choice, you are incapable of seeing possibilities.

Me: That's what I realized. If I am incapable of seeing my choices in this small example from my life, how could I have ever claimed to be an entrepreneur, someone who manifests possibilities?

Virgil: The most important word you've used today is "orienting." What is the center that you orient toward? Toward what are you orienting your actions and pursuits? The great mistake most entrepreneurs make is that they orient toward their product and lose sight of their center. They stop seeing. Without a center they are buffeted about and torn apart by the forces of the market. They fix on an idea and blind themselves to the fluid and dynamic nature of business. This is the difference between having a vision for a business or merely an idea for a product. Most entrepreneurs confuse the two. A product vision is useless unless it exists within a greater business vision.

Me: That is a great description of me when I first contacted you: torn apart. No vision.

Virgil: Without a center, no one can withstand the forces of a rapidly moving market. Like most people who call themselves entrepreneurs, you were fixed on an outcome, oriented toward a product. You couldn't see your choices.

Me: And my relationship with choice orients me to a center?

Virgil: Not just any center: your center. You are choosing. You are creating from your cen-

ter through the choices you make every moment. And when you are consciously choosing, the forces can buffet you; they can pull
and push. But you are rooted yet flexible,
powerful yet non-resistant. When you are in
choice, you can see the available opportunities
to serve your center, your ideal.

I had to sit with that for a moment. I was thinking about
my anger and my resistance and how off-center I felt
throughout the collapse of my business and the months that
followed. I was running around putting out fires, totally
reacting to the crisis of the moment. I was lost without
a center. I was blaming everyone for my shortcomings. I
wondered if I really understood what was at my center?
I wondered if I knew what was at the heart of my idea?
Then, this popped onto the screen:

Virgil: Business, like all things worth doing, is
a relationship. Relationships are never static;
they are never fixed. They change and grow
constantly. Relationships are never "known,"
they are experienced. A business is not a product just as a product is not a business. You
will know your center when you stop thinking
of things in terms of objects and start seeing
them as they are: relationships.

The Seventh Recognition: You are always in choice

Study: Identify when you tell yourself Blame stories (when do you tell stories of things happening to you?). Identify when do you tell yourself stories of Choice (when do you tell stories of making things happen?). What patterns emerge? Do you tell Blame stories in specific circumstances or when you assume specific roles?

Action: Listen to the conversations happening around you - at work, at home, on the radio, the news . . . . How often do your hear stories of blame? How often do you hear stories of choice? What's the ratio of blame stories to choice stories? Make two lists: 1) Gather language: what words are consistently used in blame stories? What phrases do you hear again and again? 2) Gather words and phrases used in choice stories. Compare your lists.

Exercise: Listen to the conversation happening within you. Using the words from the two lists in the Action step above, eliminate blame words from your inner monologue vocabulary. Replace them with the words and phrases from the choice list. Make a game of using the words from the choice list.

Recognition 8: You choose your point of view

39.

Virgil asked me to work with my relationship with choice for several weeks before approaching the last two recognitions. He told me that the final two recognitions were so obvious as to be almost invisible and I wouldn't be able to see them until I was fully living in choice. He told me that the last two recognitions are really the only two choices that we ever have.

We kept in touch. I reported what I was learning and recounted my experiences from the week or the revelations I was having. He'd ask a few questions to help me see.

And then one day while I was working there was a knock on the door. It was a special delivery. I signed for the envelope. I opened it and found this quote:

"We often need to lose sight of our priorities in order to see them." John Irving

A moment later Virgil opened a chat window and wrote:

Virgil: Do you have a minute?

Me: Yes. Did you just have an envelope delivered to my door?

Virgil: What? Don't be silly. I have a question and an exercise for you. This is your introduction to the eighth recognition. First, the question: Now that you are conscious of your relationship with choice and you are actively creating, do you know upon which mountain are you standing?

Me: What? You lost me. Is this a metaphor?

Virgil: Of course it is a metaphor! And it is also quite literal: From what point of view are you asking questions about your life, business and creativity? From what point of view are you making your choices? No need to answer now; think on it and tell me later what you discover.

Me: Okay. In case you are wondering, I am, in this moment, standing fully in "not knowing." I am oriented to choice. If I am not standing on the mountain of choice then I don't have the slightest idea where to start.

Virgil: I anticipated your lost-ness, so to help you along in your exploration, do this exercise: On a piece of paper draw a big triangle - a mountain. Next, review your journals, lists, revelations from our exercises and your practices. Gather all you know about your relationship with control and choice and revisit all relevant beliefs and assumptions. What themes, insights and judgments do you see? What labels and roles do you layer on yourself (good enough or not good enough, lacking or abundant, resilient or fragile, adventurous, entrepreneur, son, friend...)? Write the labels, themes, insights and judgments in the triangle. Now, draw a small stick figure (this is you) standing on top of the mountain.

Me: Ah. My mountain is my lens.

Virgil: The mountain is your history. This mountain is your point of view. Each of us stands on a mountain of experiences, memories, beliefs, assumptions, and interpretations. From this place we make sense of the world. From this place we interpret the immediate moment and story ourselves into the future. From this place we make our choices. Even when oriented to choice, the possibilities we see are largely determined by the labels we maintain inside the mountain. From the top of your mountain, standing on the top of all of those labels, roles, and beliefs, what do you see?

Me: Is there something specific I should be looking for?

Virgil: Nice try! Let me know what you discover.

The chat window closed.

40.

Every ending is a beginning. It is relative; it depends upon where you stand. When Parcival entered the Grail Castle the second time, was it the end of the story or a beginning? When my business collapsed, I thought it was the end and it turns out, from this vantage point, from where I stand right now, it was the threshold to what I really want to create.

For Parcival, upon asking the question, "Whom does the grail serve?" everyone in the great hall erupted in a riotous cheer, hats flew into the air, hugs and dances were had by all. The ground shook and a brilliant light radiated into the sky. Miles away, at Camelot, the Merlin calmed the frightened court. He told them that the grail had been found and the enchantment was finally lifted from the land. Here's the interesting part though: upon hearing the Merlin's words all of the knights of the Round Table, including Arthur, left Camelot. Their quest was to find Parcival.

In that moment, Parcival became the Grail King; metaphorically, he became the grail. He fulfilled himself. He became whole. The story tells us that the Fisher King taught Parcival some secret words, a prayer of sorts, and then left this world. In some traditions he ascends, in others he disappears into the forest. The healed king replaces the wounded king. It's a metaphor: to be whole you must speak your truth and own your choices.

Parcival claimed his inheritance, his ancestry, and his truth, not as the great fool, the trickster whose impulses are wild, and not as the warrior knight whose impulses are bound, suppressed in rules and doctrine. He found the middle way. He honored his nature as a human being, his need for relationship, intuition, impulse and feelings, and then reconciled them with the demands of the intellect, of hard reason, empirical data and the bottom line.

The story is a story of balance restored. It is a story of seeing what is there and not what you think is there. Parc-i-val, means the middle way, the arrow that shoots through the center of two opposites.

When he became the Grail King, for the first time in his life, Parcival could see beyond his story. He could see options and opportunities. He was no longer a seeker. He was a seer. As Virgil would probably say, that would seem to be an important skill for an entrepreneur. Wouldn't you agree?

41.

I remember as a kid learning about perspective. I took some drawing classes at the local recreation center. We first learned to draw single point perspective: all lines meet at a single spot on the horizon called the vanishing point. In our simple drawings, roads and train tracks ran toward the vanishing point. Telephone poles and barns all followed the lines and disappeared into a single point. Technically, that point is meant to draw the eye to it, to pull your eye into the drawing. It is the organizing principle of sight.

I remember, as I was drawing my single point perspective drawings, even as a kid I knew there were greater implications. It was a cool trick to create the illusion of distance on a two dimensional piece of paper. I was fascinated by the idea that single point perspective drawings actually required two points to be meaningful: the vanishing point on the horizon and me. I was the other point. Someone needed to look into the paper and see the illusion of distance. A drawing requires a looker, a participant, to be complete. I drew it. I also looked into it. If drawing the picture was a creative act, then looking into it was also an act of creation. The illusion was of my creation.

I drew my mountain as Virgil suggested (a triangle) and filled it in with all of the labels and words that I use to describe my learning. I added my purpose and vision statements and mission statements and any other words I use to define my business and my life. I realized how many of my assumptions come from my family, my ancestry, and my culture. In filling in the mountain I was discovering the source of my seeing.

After I completed filling in my mountain, I drew a little stick figure (me) on top. That's when I remembered doing perspective drawings as a boy. I realized that the stick figure on the mountain and the "someone looking into the illusion" of my perspective drawing were essentially the same thing.

The previous recognitions taught me that I was telling myself a story. They taught me that I could change my story. They taught me that, just like the drawings, my illusion was of my creation. They taught me that I am in choice every minute of my life.

Virgil asked me to continue adding to the lists so I might further develop a practice of letting go what I can't control. A benefit of doing the control exercise is that I realized that I could never occupy another person's point of view. I would never be able to see through another person's eyes nor would anyone be able to see through my eyes: perspective is personal and unique. My mountain was mine. My point of view was always going to be uniquely mine. Other people were standing on their own mountains seeing from their own unique perspective.

Virgil wrote that the final two recognitions were:

- So obvious as to be almost invisible
- I wouldn't be able to see them until I was fully living in choice

- The final two recognitions are really the only two choices that we ever have

It was glaringly obvious: I choose my perspective. I choose where I stand relative to what I want. I choose how I define my view from the top of my mountain.

The next day I met Elizabeth for lunch. I'd not seen her since she gave me Virgil's contact information many months ago. I was telling her about my remembrance of perspective drawing and she smiled, saying, "So, you've made it to the eighth recognition."

I smiled, too, and said, "You were right. Aren't you glad that I contacted Virgil and that we're not having the same old conversation yet another time?"

She nodded and said, "I love the term, 'vanishing point!' There's a whole world happening beyond that point and we just can't see it." She seemed lost in thought for a moment and then exclaimed, "You know, it is beyond the vanishing point that everything is possible."

"Yes, that's really the point of the drawing, isn't it?" I said. "A perspective drawing begins with a horizon line. A horizon begs you to imagine what's beyond. Add a dot on the horizon and it begs you to step toward it! Make all lines run to the dot and you just have to step into the drawing and follow the lines to see where they go."

Elizabeth said quietly, "Most people fear the vanishing point. They fear its call. So they pretend that the vanishing point is an anchor useful in making their picture seem more real. They want their illusion and they want others to see the picture the way they see it. They want to stand in a fixed point and never move. They stand safe and secure on their perch and look into the picture. And from their perch they search for meaning instead of stepping into it. The meaning is in the step."

I was quiet for a moment. Elizabeth added, "Do you recognize how unusual you are in your desire to step into the picture? How important it is that you recognize your desire and willingness to step toward the vanishing point? That desire to step is the very quality that makes you an entrepreneur. The whole point is not *what* you see, but *how* you see."

She was right. When you walk toward the vanishing point, you have no idea what is beyond it. In Virgil-speak, to step into the picture is the whole point of practicing "not knowing." The need to know impedes the capacity to walk into possibilities. I realized in my conversation with Elizabeth, that the real vitality of life always lies in the direction of the vanishing point. We stand in the present, in the foreground of the picture. It is the mountain; it is the point of view. Literally. It is the point from which I view. I can stand in fixed point as a witness or I can step as a participant dynamically into a picture that will change the moment I step into it. My point of view can be fluid, moving as I move, moving as the picture moves.

I can orient my choices according to a fixed point of view

(an observer). I can orient my choices according to a fluid point of view (a participant).

Either way, it is a choice. I choose my perspective. I am oriented to choice and my choices are sourced from my point of view. I can follow the most natural human impulse and say, "I wonder what's over that hill?" In this way I practice stepping into the unknown. Or, I can say, as most people have learned to do, "I need to know before I begin walking." In which case, they rarely, if ever, leave their perch.

42.

At our next chat I shared with Virgil my thoughts and my conversation with Elizabeth. This is what he wrote in response:

> **Virgil:** As I wrote earlier, each of us stands on a mountain of experiences, memories, beliefs, assumptions, and interpretations. This mountain is our history. This mountain is our point of view. From this place we make sense of the world. From this place we interpret the immediate moment and story ourselves into the future. The possibilities we see are largely determined by the labels we maintain inside the mountain.

Most of us are standing on a mountain that defines us as separate from our fulfillment. We stand on our mountain and our fulfillment is some other place - in the future or the past, in the eyes, thoughts and expectations of another person, in a number in a bank account. Because our fulfillment is some other place, this mountain can seem like it is missing a piece, like it is empty, chaotic, deficient or somehow lacking in meaning. In your words, it is a fixed point of view, the perch of an observer who is separate from his fulfillment.

From the mountain of separation our fulfillment will always look like a distant meadow. Even when we achieve "it," it can never be what we imagined. Fulfillment is not an outcome to be achieved. It is not a place "out there" somewhere, but instead is a relationship sourced from within. It is fluid. It moves with you, as you.

When we look to the next peak to find our fulfillment, we invest our satisfaction in the new gadget, the new car, the next job, the new relationship, the next business and although we might experience temporary satisfaction, true fulfillment evaporates. Sooner or later we learn that what we seek isn't on the next peak;

what we seek is inside the mountain upon which we are standing. We necessarily begin looking inside the mountain.

Where there is separation outside, there is separation inside; in fact, we see separation outside because we've created internal separation. It turns out that your point of view is the point! Among the first separations we generate as we grow up is the separation from our creative identity. Our creative identity is more than the artistic impulse. It is:

- the experience of having impact

- knowing that your thoughts and actions matter

- knowing that your thoughts and actions literally create the world you embody

This separation is at the heart of your relationship with choice: Do you truly know that you make things happen or are your choices made according to the point of view of "things happening to you?" As you discovered, these are two distinctly different orientations to the world and as it turns out, how you orient (your point of view) is what determines whether you see though the eyes of an entrepreneur or through the eyes of an everyman.

As I suggested earlier, you only really have two choices and the first choice is how you choose to orient yourself to your story and your world. Are you an observer (fixed) or a participant (fluid)? Are you separate from your fulfillment (fixed) or are you the creator of your fulfillment (fluid)? This choice is your point of view.

The Eighth Recognition: You choose your point of view

Study: Locate your mountain. Identify the mountain upon which you perceive the world. Draw a triangle and fill it in with all the labels and roles you apply to your life. What informs your point of view?

Action: Play with your point of view. Ask five friends to describe your strengths. Listen without responding. What do they describe that surprises you?

Exercise: Imagine it is your birthday, a landmark event sometime in the future. There are many people attending who have come to thank you for something you created or a service you provided. For what do they thank you? Specifically? Define the actions that take you from this day to that birthday event. Identify the first step. Take it.

Recognition 9: You choose where you place your focus

43.

This week Virgil wrote that most people in business are hungry ghosts and that when I first came to him, I too was a hungry ghost. I wasn't familiar with the term and so he sent this from Wikipedia:

> **Virgil**: Hungry ghosts ". . . are represented as teardrop or paisley-shaped with bloated stom-

achs and necks too thin to pass food such that attempting to eat is also incredibly painful. Some are described as having "mouths the size of a needle's eye and a stomach the size of a mountain." This is a metaphor for people "futilely attempting to fulfill their illusory physical desires." In the Japanese tradition there is a version of hungry ghost known as a gaki. Gaki ". . . are the spirits of. . . greedy people who, as punishment for their mortal vices, have been cursed with an insatiable hunger for a particular substance or object."

I protested and wrote:

Me: How was I a hungry ghost? What was I greedy for?

Virgil: You were chasing an illusion. You could not see what was right in front of you.

Me: My business had collapsed. I was scared and desperate.

Virgil: Exactly. You wanted success for yourself but lost sight entirely of the people you serve, also known as your customers. And you thought yourself a failure and that further blinded you. Most people in business quickly forget what business they are in. They lose sight of their purpose and focus on their product or their paycheck. Their actions disconnect from their reason for acting! Can you deny that this was true of you?

Me: No . . .

Virgil: My reflections are not accusations. Remember, your experiences are good lessons if you suspend judgment and I am not judging you. I am introducing you to the final recognition. When you contacted me you had the everyman idea that you could not act until you knew what to do. You had to know. We flipped that notion so you now see that vitality and true entrepreneurship live in the direction of "not knowing." Now you've chosen a different point of view. In fact, you have returned to the most natural human point of view: curiosity, stepping toward the vanishing point, in no way separate from any part of yourself. We've performed another flip in that you are no longer reacting to your circumstances but making clear choices. You are conscious of the lens through which you see the world and the story you subsequently tell from your unique point of view. True?

Me: Yes. I feel like I am an entirely different person.

Virgil: You are. You are no longer oriented to the story that things happen to you. You are now oriented to the story that you make things happen. This is another flip!

Me: Yes. Even the way I organize my day is now totally different. It feels as if I am moving slower yet I am getting much more accomplished.

Virgil: You are no longer a hungry ghost. You are no longer in the world according to what you can get from it. You are now oriented according to what you bring to it. Yet > another flip! Do you recognize how these "flips" have changed how you see?

Me: I find that I am aware of my assumptions. I find that I can suspend my assumptions, (some of the time ;-)) and that allows me to see beyond what I think is there. I feel as if I am not getting in my own way - my anger, my frustration, my running around putting out fires . . . . all of those actions are wasted energy.

Virgil: And now you are ready for the final recognition. This is the subtlest of all the recognitions and has been available to you all along. It is also perhaps the most potent. For the ninth recognition we loop back to the very beginning. What was the first thing? What did I ask you to do?

Me: You asked me to focus on my patterns. You asked me to recognize that I didn't have problems but that I had patterns.

Virgil: And what did you do as a first step?

Me: I took a walk because I was angry. And during my walk, I began looking for and seeing patterns. They were everywhere.

Virgil: So, take a walk. Follow the same route you took on the first day. Look at patterns.

Look at how you look. Tell me what you
discover in our next chat.

44.

I took my walk and saw nothing new that illuminated
the ninth recognition. I saw patterns. I was present. I was
missing something.

The next day I had a few calls in the morning and then
met my friend Dwight for coffee. I was early so I sat at my
table and read a book on my iPad when the conversation
at the next table caught my attention. Two teachers were
talking about working with their students. One, a vibrant
older woman with sparkling blue eyes, was mentoring the
other, an eager young man in his early twenties. They were
talking about belief.

She said, "The students often tell me what they can't do.
They say, 'Oh, I'll never be able to do math or climb a
mountain . . .' They only see what they can't do."

"How do you handle that?" he asked and she smiled.

"I learned a long time ago not to resist their disbelief."
The young man looked puzzled and the woman laughed.
"Resisting their point of view only makes them hang onto
their belief. Their world is populated by adults who tell
them, 'You can do anything!' They know it isn't true. So, I
don't resist their belief or try to change it."

The young man was visibly confused and said, "But how do we encourage them if we don't try and change their belief?"

The older woman took a sip of her coffee and responded, "Only they can change their belief. I don't see their limits, they do. So I help them change what they see."

"How?" the young man challenged.

I giggled because he reminded me of how I initially worked with Virgil.

She said, "I say to them, 'Okay, let's agree that right now you can't do it. Let's pretend for a moment that you could do it. What would you do if you could? What would be your first step?'" She took another sip of her coffee and then continued, "They always have ideas of the first step so I tell them to take that step. They don't need to believe that they can or can't do anything. They only need to see one simple step, see what is right in front of them, and act as if . . . ."

And then she said something that made me spit out my coffee. She sat back and said, "Belief comes second. They don't need to believe, they need to take a step. If their focus is on their belief or lack of belief, they'll freeze. Ask them, 'What if . . .' and their focus shifts immediately. They see a step, not a belief. They can take a step. It's do-able. Then another. And another. And one day they are doing the thing that they thought impossible. It all depends on where they place their focus."

Dwight joined me at the table as I typed into my iPad. Belief comes second. Focus on the action. "What if . . . ."

Dwight had just returned from vacation. He was tanned and relaxed and excited to tell me a story. He said, "You're going to get this! You of all people are going to get this!" Several months before when I was working through the initial recognitions I tried to explain the concept of "not knowing" to Dwight and he nearly blew a fuse. How do you explain the recognitions over lunch? I'd learned with Dwight it was better not to try.

He is a new but avid diver and during his vacation he did a night dive. Listening to his story my mouth dropped open. It was as if Virgil sent a one-two punch in the form of the teachers and then Dwight to illuminate the ninth recognition for me. I laughed out loud in the middle of his story. He was taken aback and I explained that he'd just solved a mystery for me and I asked him to please continue. This is the story Dwight told me:

> "It was a really dark night. I was ninety feet below the surface of the water - deep! I was really frightened and I tried to slow my breathing so the air in my tanks would last a little longer. I didn't want to burn through all of my air because I was scared. We were diving in the belly of a ship that sank before I was born. This was my first wreck dive *and* my first night dive. I kept telling myself, "You are an idiot! What are you doing? Idiot!" My whole focus

was on my fear and I was trying to focus on my breathing to calm myself down.

The beam of my flashlight cut a path through the darkest dark I have ever known. Once, many years ago, I was in a cave and the guide turned out the lights so we could experience the absence of light. Man, that was dark - but this underwater dark was darker. It was like the water gave weight to the blackness. I kept trying to slow my breath, move my focus away from my fear.

As I was working to calm myself I realized that I could see only where I pointed my light. That sounds simplistic but it was a revelation for me. I could only see what was in my beam and I interpreted what I saw in the beam: I heard myself say things like "beautiful," or "odd," or "scary." It occurred to me that this is true no matter where I am or what I am doing. It was what I was doing in my fear! I see only where I point my light and I was pointing my light at fear so that's what I saw!

Isn't that just like everyday? It's just like life! I see where I point my light. And, here's the other thing, just like my flashlight beam, my focus is really narrow! I don't see all that is

there. I see this narrow beam and interpret
everything I see according to what I believe.

This is the point when I laughed. I apologized and asked
him to continue. He said:

> In the belly of that shipwreck I began to under-
> stand the power of where I place my focus. I
> instantly settled down. My breathing calmed,
> and I started to enjoy the dive. I wasn't looking
> at my fear; I focused on what was in my beam
> and how I was choosing to interpret what I
> saw in the beam.

I could already hear Virgil's voice: Where you point your
focus is a choice and your focus is narrow. You only see
what you illuminate, you interpret what is in your beam.
Belief follows.

That was the ninth recognition: I choose where I place my
focus.

45.

I took a walk. I shined the flashlight of my focus on the
many patterns that I saw in my neighborhood. I realized
that, since my first conversation with Virgil, it was almost
impossible for me not to see patterns. I was now asking

myself a lot more questions like, "What if . . . ?" instead of making absolute statements, "This means this!"

I pointed my focus and listened to my interpretation recognizing that I was interpreting. I was not seeing fact or a reality that existed outside of my seeing. I was capable of pivoting if circumstances changed. I was nimble and fluid and creating.

When I returned to my house, just as happened after my first walk, I found a note taped to my door.

"Remember tonight. . . for it is the beginning of always."

Dante Alighieri

46.

It was our final chat. I told Virgil about the teachers and Dwight's dive experience and how they helped me see the ninth recognition. I told him I thought the earth would shake and the heavens would part when I achieved the ninth recognition. Now I understood that not only does it close the loop called Choice, but as he mentioned, it loops back to the where we started. He reiterated that there is not "end" or "an achievement," but rather ours was a game of mastery. We were playing to become better players.

He finished our chat with these thoughts:

> **Virgil**: Choosing where you place your focus
> is one of the most powerful choices you can

make. It can be life changing. And, it is always understated.

Significant change is often subtle. It does not come with fireworks and a brass band. It's a paradox. Big change slips in unannounced - usually after all the drama is finished. Choosing where you place your focus seems straightforward, like removing your sunglasses, yet initially you have to intend it. You have to choose it over and over again and in the choosing you are creating a new pattern of seeing. When your perception begins to shift you begin to see things in a different way. You begin to see life through a different lens so you begin to create a different life.

Pattern. Story. Choice. These three circles guide us to a renewed relationship with Seeing. I say "renewed" because we are born capable of seeing but then lose our sight amidst the story we acquire and tell.

Changing your relationship with Seeing is choosing to look at life through a different lens. Again, it sounds simple but is often tricky precisely because the shift is so subtle. It is easy to say, "Change where you place your focus; change the lens through which you see," and it's another matter to actually do the consistent work of re- patterning necessary to choose your focus and be conscious of your interpretation.

As I've said, entrepreneurs are like artists. When young artists work on proper technique they necessarily must challenge old patterns. Often what feels "right" is a bad habit that limits their artistry. The new pattern, learning proper technique, feels awkward and forced until it is habituated. The new pattern needs to be embodied - put into the body. It is a change in the body and only superficially an exercise of the intellect. For instance, many actors and singers need to learn how to breathe properly. The intention begins as a thought but the real work happens in the body. Learning to place your focus is a similar process. As a child, the first time you learned to place your focus, you were not conscious of what you were doing, just as the young artist was not aware that he was developing shallow breathing patterns. It was all you knew to do and so you reinforced a pattern until it was integrated in your body.

So, there will be no fanfare. Living in choice will bring internal transformations that may not be immediately apparent in the day-to-day activities of your life. The people around you might sense a difference. They'll think that you changed your hair, your style of clothes or suspect that you have a secret. Rarely do the day-to-day actions in your life change but how you do them is different. You are changed within the circumstances of your life.

You are now able to stand solidly in the chaos without needing to control it, contain it, or deny it. You are capable of being present without needing to manipulate anything or anyone. You can say without inhibition exactly what you need to say without the need to please or edit yourself. You can give voice to what is appropriate for you despite what others might think.

You are choosing where you stand. You are choosing where you aim your focus, you are choosing how you interpret what you see, and you are choosing the actions you take. You are seeing.

You are focused on what you bring to business, not on what you get from it. Now, you are an entrepreneur.

The Ninth Recognition: You choose where you place your focus

Study: Study your focus placement. Do you see problems or opportunities? Do you see obstacles or potentials? For a day, track where you place your focus. Pay attention to what you give your attention.

Action: Describe in word or image (the more specific you can be, the better): what in your life energizes you? What feeds your spirit? What is your passion? How much of your focus do you give to things that deplete you? How much focus do you give to things that energize you?

Exercise: Using the description from above, consider this: What if your passion, the thing that feeds your spirit, was not something you seek but instead was something that you bring to your experiences. Describe in image and word, the more specific the better, how the small moments in your life would change if you were responsible for bringing energy and passion to your life instead of chasing after your passions? Describe what you might do differently when oriented according to what you bring? Choose one thing. Do it.

Epilogue

We were at lunch. I knew why we were there. Her business was in serious trouble. I met Sarah at a conference three years before when both of our businesses were failing. Since then I was fulfilling my aspirations. I had more clients than ever before. My line of products was booming. I was now exploring options in software development. I was ready to scale-up my business.

Sarah confessed her frustration and fear to me. "I need to do something different." She put her head in her hands. "Why can't I see what I'm doing wrong?" she sighed.

I smiled and folded my hands, "We've had this conversation before," I said. "A couple of times. Do you remember?"

"Of course I remember," she said, averting her eyes. She moved her water glass like a chess piece.

"We can have this same conversation again in a few years if you want. Or, you can do what I suggested the last time we had it. Contact Virgil," I said. I wrote an email address on a slip of paper and slid it across the table to her.

"Who is this guy?" she stared at the paper. "Why are you so insistent that I contact him?"

"He can help you," I smiled. I made sure I had eye contact. I wanted her to know how important it was for her to contact Virgil. "He helped me. He can help you, too, if you are ready."

"What do you mean, 'If I'm ready?'" she wrinkled her brow.

"Contact him and find out. Or, do what you always do and we can have lunch again in a year and have this same conversation over again. The real question here is are you frustrated enough to change what you are doing?"

A Note About The Maps

It goes without saying that The Seer is a narrative draped over a specific geography of concepts. In other words, it is more teaching than storytelling. Although Virgil would never approve, I've decided to provide a few maps to better navigate the territory. Everything is clearer from elevation and that is the purpose of Maps 1 & 2, to provide a birds eye view of the geography.

A great teacher once taught me that artistry was not about doing, but about seeing. Specifically, it was about seeing what was there and not what I thought was there. Once the artist can see beyond the limits of their thinking, they can help others see, too. Having your eyes and mind opened often feels like a perceptual flip – because it is. The mindset of the entrepreneur and the mindset of the artist are remarkably similar: an entrepreneur, like an artist, needs to develop the capacity to see what others do not or cannot see. The three cycles of this book (pattern, story, choice) are the epicenters of the perceptual flips necessary to SEE. Map #3 makes explicit the flips.

Map 4 provides some insight into why I chose the images used in the book. Some carry history, some a personal reference, and some are simply cool images that I wanted to use.

Each Recognition chapter comes with a quote. If I were

forced to give a short summary of the book, I'd hand over the quotes. So, I thought it might be useful to see the quotes in sequence and that is Map 5.

Map 1: Practices and Concepts

Cycle One: Pattern

Recognition 1: You don't have a problem. You have a pattern

Practice: Practice Not Knowing (curiosity)

Concept: Stories stalk you

Recognition 2: Your language matters

Practice: Orient according to the question (not the answer)

Concept: Problem seeing = mechanistic; Pattern seeing = relational

Recognition 3: You are telling yourself a story

Practice: Distinguish between your circumstance and your story

Concept: Significant change happens through simplicity, not complexity

Cycle Two: Story

Recognition 4: You locate yourself within your story

Practice: Learn to have the experience first and make meaning second

Concept: Suspend judgments and learn

Recognition 5: You are the teller of your story

Practice: Challenge your self-imposed limitations (Premature Cognitive Commitment)

Concept: Separations (self from self)

Recognition 6: You can change your story

Practice: Distinguish between what you can and can't control

Concept: The relationship between control and choice

Cycle Three: Choice

Recognition 7: You are always in choice

Practice: Distinguish between stories of choice and stories of blame

Concept: Responsibility and ownership

Recognition 8: You choose your point of view

Practice: Stand on the mountain - see what informs your point of view

Concept: Fixed and Fluid P.O.V (vanishing point and stepping into unknowns)

Recognition 9: You choose where you place your focus

Concept: Orient according to what you bring, not what you get

Concept: Belief follows experience

Map 2: Study, Action, and Exercise Alignment

Cycle One: Pattern

Recognition 1: You don't have a problem. You have a pattern

Study: Identify pattern

Action: Play with pattern

Exercise: Discern patterns within and without (self)

Recognition 2: Your language matters

Study: Identify pattern in word

Action: Play with language use (words)

Exercise: Discern patterns in the language of others (other)

Recognition 3: You are telling yourself a story

Study: Identify pattern in story

Action: Play with story

Exercise: Discern the story patterns (self and other)

Cycle Two: Story

Recognition 4: You locate yourself within your story

Study: Locate role/investments

Action: Play with meaning making

Exercise: Challenge your judgments

Recognition 5: You are the teller of your story

Study: Locate action

Action: Play with being the meaning maker

Exercise: Challenge your limits

Recognition 6: You can change your story

Study: Locate target + useful action

Action: Play with intentional meaning making

Exercise: Challenge your control

Cycle Three: Choice

Recognition 7: You are always in choice

Study: Discover assumption

Action: Play with assumptions

Exercise: Choose your assumption

Recognition 8: You choose your point of view

Study: Discover point of view

Action: Play with point of view

Exercise: Choose your point of view

Recognition 9: You choose where you place your focus

Study: Discover focus placement

Action: Play with focus placement

Exercise: Choose your focus

Map 3: Concept Flips

First Cycle: Pattern

From needing to know to not knowing (orient according to curiosity)

Second Cycle: Story

From "Things happen to me" to "I make things happen" (orient according to choice)

Third Cycle: Choice

From witness to creator (orient according to what you bring)

Overall (Spine)

Have the experience first and make meaning second

Map 4: Images

Prologue

Photo: LOOK sign

Sometimes I carry a pocket camera with me, not to capture events of the day or landscapes, but because it helps me "see." I go into the world looking for small things, the stuff I take for granted or pass without really noticing. For a while I was interested in the symbols and markings on the street. They are everywhere. Since this book is about learning to see I thought this particular symbol that came from my practice of "seeing" was most appropriate for the prologue.

Cycle One: Pattern

Photo: Westlake Sculpture Installation: Borders by Steinunn Thorarinsdottir, featuring 26 aluminum and cast iron sculptures

I keep a visual inspiration file. One day, while walking across downtown Seattle, I came upon a fantastic installation at Westlake Center by XX. It stopped me in my tracks and

I spent several moments wandering through and appreciating the sculptures. One of the themes that I gleaned was the pattern of isolation and non-communication in an urban landscape: feeling alone in a city of a million people. I liked this photo because of the face-to-face position of the sculptures, fists clenched in isolation, and the many supporting patterns apparent in bricks and buildings.

First Recognition: You don't have a problem. You have a pattern

Photo: Cross Walk Man

Near the King Street rail station in Seattle is pedestrian bridge meant to guide travelers from the train to the buses and light rail available in the nearby International District. A pattern of yellow cross walk men mark the path from station to bridge. They remind me of hustling commuters, each locked in their personal mission and unaware that they are part of a greater pattern.

Second Recognition: Your language matters

Wordle from The Direction of Intention

My friend Mark dumped my blog (all 725 posts) into Wordle and this is the image that it created. The biggest words are the most often used in my writing. I like this image because I think the same process is in play with the language we use in our lives: the world we see is dependent upon by the words we use most in the story we tell.

Third Recognition: You are telling yourself a story

Painting: The Poet

I did this painting for my friend Sam. He is a brilliant poet who for years hid his poems because he told himself the story that they weren't good enough. After cajoling him for weeks he finally slipped me a folder of his poems. They are brilliant and I'm happy to say he's changed his story and has published his work under the title Fully Human.

Cycle Two: Story

Painting: The Elders

Many years ago I took a class called Art and Transformation. We studied different cultures and processes of transformation as the impulse driving visual forms. I realized during the course that "story" was central to transformation. Art is meant to be the keeper and transformer of identity and identity is nothing more than a story. This painting comes from my work in that class.

Fourth Recognition: You locate yourself within your story

Painting: Solo Dancer

This is the most recent painting of the series in the book. For many months I'd been bored with my painting (sure sign of a coming growth phase) and was experimenting with new surfaces and techniques. This is the painting where all the experimentation came together. It landed and I was no longer wandering but had found my new artistic location. Just as I now locate myself within this arena, we are constantly locating ourselves in our lives; we physically locate ourselves in space (where do you like to sit when you go to the movies?) and we metaphorically locate ourselves in our lives. "Comfort zone" is a term of location, as is "preference" as is "community." Some locations are given, others are chosen, most are patterned.

Fifth Recognition: You are the teller of your story

Photo: Shadow Play

I love shadows - literally and metaphorically. Most stories are about people walking into their fears and fears lurk in the shadows. Shadow work leads to an inevitable realization: you create the fear because you tell the story. Recognizing that you are the teller of your own story, the interpreter of your experience, is great for releasing shadows.

Sixth Recognition: You can change your story

Photo: Megan's Foot

Megan and I were walking along Alki Beach when we came upon this foot drawn in the sand. She put her foot within the sand drawing and said, "This guy must be huge!" She looked around for the giant who was nowhere to be found. One purpose of imagination is to entertain possibilities. Changing a story begins with entertaining possibilities - just like entrepreneurship!

Cycle Three: Choice

Illustration: Play to Play

This is from a yet-to-be-published children's book I wrote and illustrated based on James Carse's book, Finite And Infinite Games. The gorilla and the girl want to play but first must understand what that means: are they playing to win or playing to play. It's to make a choice: one path leads to mastery and the other leads to temporary gratification (or despair). The power is in the choice.

Seventh Recognition: You are always in choice

Photo: Street Arrow

I write a blog called The Direction of Intention. The title comes from a term I learned in the theatre: are you going to push against what you don't want or walk toward what you want to create. The Direction of Intention is the first choice point in any creative process. Which way will you go?

Cartoons - Salesman/Caveman

I've always drawn cartoons. I scribble

them on envelops, draw them on birthday cards. I wrote the image into the books so I could scribble a few.

Eighth Recognition: You choose your point of view

Painting: Pigeon Pier

One early morning Alan and I walked the beach on Long Island Sound. We walked out onto a pier and suddenly the pier vibrated alive with sound. Underneath were hundreds of pigeons and we must have startled them into life. Their cooing shook the pier. It was so unexpected that it felt as if we entered a new and magical world. We stood there for several minutes and enjoyed the sound bath. Later we talked about how the experience jolted us into presence; the magic was there all along.

Ninth Recognition: You choose where you place your focus

Painting: Eve

Mythologically, Eve and Pandora are the same figure. They introduce human kind into the field of dualities. Knowledge is only available through contrast. In contrast resides the most fundamental choice: where are you going to place your focus. Are you going to look to the heavens and ask, "How could you do this to me," or are you going to look to yourself and ask, "What do I want to do?"

Epilogue

Photo: Spiral in the sand

This is another sand drawing found near the giant foot. Spirals are often symbolic of infinity and a good symbol for flipping from seeker to seer. A seer is only useful when passing on the wisdom.

Map 5: Quotes

Recognition 1: You don't have a problem. You have a pattern

"Thought is the sculptor who can create the person you want to be."

Henry David Thoreau

Recognition 2: Your language matters

"One must be leery of words because words turn into cages."

Viola Spolin

Recognition 3: You are telling yourself a story

"People take on the shapes of the songs and the stories that surround them, especially if they don't have their own song."

Neil Gaiman

Recognition 4: You locate yourself within your story

"Experience is not what happens to you; it's what you do with what happens to you."

Aldous Huxley

Recognition 5: You are the teller of your story

"The story of the human race is the story of men and women selling themselves short."

Abraham Maslow

Recognition 6: You can change your story

"The snake which cannot cast its skin has to die. As well the minds which are prevented from changing their opinions; they cease to be a mind."

Friedrich Nietzsche

Recognition 7: You are always in choice

"It's not our talents that make us safe or dangerous, it's our choices."

Josephine Angelini, Dreamless

Recognition 8: You choose your point of view

"We often need to lose sight of our priorities in order to see them."

John Irving

Recognition 9: You choose where you place your focus

"Remember tonight. . . for it is the beginning of always."

Dante Alighieri

Afterward

On a sunny spring day a year ago, I was one of the organizers for a joint academic, corporate, and government workshop at the University of Washington in Bothell focused on 21st century learning. Since most of the participants did not know each other, we wanted to spend the first morning in non-traditional "get to know you" exercises. One of the other organizers knew of David Robinson's facilitation work and suggested that David could run a couple of "kinesthetic" exercises. Little did I know at the time that I had found the future collaborator that I have looked for the past ten years.

David led us through what I've since learned is his "Angel and Devil" exercises to help us experience, through moving around the room in two different ways, what it means to "experience first and make meaning second." Most of my adult life I've reversed these steps and missed much of what happens around me. Over the last year, and intensely over the last four months while collaborating with David on this book, while teaching graduate students how to design a human centered venture and starting a new venture (Flipped StartUP), I experienced first-hand the insights, energy and difference that *The Seer* made in my life.

From the single hour that David spent coaching human centered designers to prepare for their final product pitch,

I experienced the best presentations students have ever done in my classes in twenty years. In a short time, David introduced the notion of story as a more powerful way to "bring an opportunity" to a customer or investor rather than our traditional problem/solution pitch. Watching the light bulbs go on as David shared the elegant story format of "yearning meets obstacle" was amazing to behold.

More recently, David and I tag teamed my entrepreneuring class to develop the mind of the entrepreneur. I provided the selected readings on effectual entrepreneuring from Saras Sarasvathy along with the lecture material. As part of developing the entrepreneurial mind, one of the key facets is the relationship of chaos and order. Too many designers and entrepreneurs think that their role is to see the customer chaos and create order and then they are done. They miss that customers in combination with the inexorable march of technology are constantly cycling between order and chaos.

As I worked through these concepts with the class in my left-brained way, it was clear to me that most of the class was not getting these core concepts. David and I switched places and he led the class through a diagram of chaos and order and the "angel devil" exercise followed by the triangle exercise. David engaged their kinesthetic senses to take the students quickly through the experience of chaos and order. With the experience, now embedded in each student, they were ready to make meaning. As evidenced by the in-class exercises the rest of the evening and several unsolicited emails the following day, the students got the fundamentals of the effectual entrepreneuring mindset.

Five weeks later, the students participated in a reflection exercise[2] about the journey that we had been on for the previous eight weeks of class. One of the teams generated a surprisingly deep multi-layer visual representation of their journey.

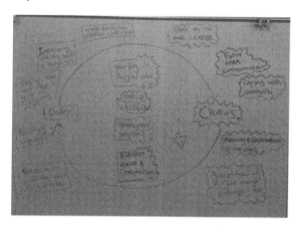

The student team reflected:

> "What is in green is what we've learned this quarter. In red are the kinds of hassles we struggled with in class. In the middle is the essence of what we've learned this quarter.

[2]http://skipwalter.net/2013/03/03/reflecting-on-effectual-entrepreneuring-pedagogy/

The 'Build and Learn' loop in the middle illustrates this cycle of having to build in order to learn something and in that build/learn process, it is not always clear what is chaos and what is order.

"We really liked the 'Chaos and Order' loop that David Robinson[3] introduced us to and how easy it is to focus on the Order and lose sight of how we need to keep coming back to the Chaos.

"At some level, the green and red text boxes on the left and right sides of the diagram represent the duality between Chaos and Order. For example, the 'pressure to build the best thing possible' is balanced with the chaos of accepting that a 'good enough' prototype early as a minimum viable product[4] will help us learn more from the customers."

The joy of seeing such an insightful diagram of the class learning process demonstrated to David and me that we were on the right track to quickly getting early stage entrepreneurs to understand how to operate in this different world which is so different from their everyday large corporation experience.

[3]http://www.trulypowerful.com/Truly_Powerful_People_Seattle_WA.html
[4]http://en.wikipedia.org/wiki/Minimum_viable_product

As David and I continued our conversation, David realized that what he had learned in art school and throughout all of his work in the theater was the same core process as what I had learned in my forty years of entrepreneuring and intrapreneuring. However, we each had different words and language and ways of describing our essential processes and fundamental concepts. We laughed when we both realized that one of the primary resources that influenced both of us was The Artist's Way at Work. Even with all the wonderful exercises in this book, understanding the essence of this point of view often requires close collaboration with a master.

David Robinson is the Master of Seeing that I have sought for forty years. His way of seeing and his way of translating the knowledge of those of us hobbled with left-brain thinking is a delight to experience. More important, it is rewarding to incorporate David's Nine Recognitions of the Entrepreneur into my consulting practice of mentoring and teaching early stage entrepreneurs.

Enjoy the journey as this master executive coach shares what it means to "see" the path of the effectual entrepreneur.

Skip Walter

March 19, 2013

About the Author

"David Robinson is a gift. If you have worked with him as a consultant, coach, facilitator, artist, director, collaborator, or performer, or have known him as a friend, then you know this already."
Alan Seale

"David Robinson is the Master of Seeing that I have sought for forty years. His way of seeing and his way of translating the knowledge of those of us hobbled with left-brain thinking is a delight to experience." *Skip Walter*

David Robinson is a visual and theatre artist. His work is rooted in story and he helps people see: their own stories, their patterns, their choices, and ultimately, their extraordinary capacity. David speaks and workshops in a wide range of arenas, including corporate, non-profit and academia, and maintains a coaching practice with individuals and groups seeking clarity and change. THE SEER joins his body of work that embraces his writing, painting, directing and his visionary heart.

Made in the USA
Lexington, KY
27 January 2014